ANWAR SADAT

ANWAR SADAT
THE LAST HUNDRED DAYS

PHOTOGRAPHS BY KONRAD MÜLLER

TEXT BY MARK BLAISSE

THE VENDOME PRESS

Book designed by Konrad R. Müller

The Vendome Press, New York

© Copyright 1981, Verlag Fritz Molden,
Wien–München–Zürich–New York

Printed and bound in Germany
Distributed by The Viking Press
625 Madison Avenue
New York, N.Y. 10022

ISBN: 0-86565-022-5

CONTENTS

I   *Ramadan*   7

II   *Sinai*   37

III   *Travels*   55

Epilogue   71

Biographical Note   75

I Ramadan

Mit Abu el Kom, the village on the Nile delta where Anwar Sadat was born. After the wild drive from Cairo it takes a long time to beat the dust out of our jackets. It is hot and humid in the large hall where an officer of the presidential guard has parked us; Sadat, usually in marshal's uniform, stares down from dozens of photographs. We had noticed the primitive portraits along the road, which make him omnipresent. Severe and stiff, eyes focused on infinity. When we are finally allowed into the garden after hours of waiting, we are not prepared for a relaxed encounter. But the man who comes towards us down the tiled path from the lemon orchard promptly dissipates many of our unconscious preconceptions. Not that his dignity suffers from his short-sleeved terrycloth shirt, matching beige shorts, white socks and American tennis shoes. His step, almost a quick march, is too military for that, as is the military stick that he clasps under his right arm like a British officer. He almost always carries this gnarled, unlikely cane. For years now, a good quick walk has been an integral part of Sadat's strict daily routine, and his muscular legs do not betray his sixty-two years. He wears large sunglasses and a straw hat to shield him from the burning sun on the path; the trees offer little protection.

"These four palm trees were given to me by the Libyan president Gaddafi. The only present he ever gave me, the dangerous fool." He points with his cane to the trees, laughs and wipes the perspiration from his forehead with a tissue. He has to take his glasses off to do this, and we can see his eyes. They look calm, a bit tired from the physical hardship of two weeks of fasting. Ramadan, which falls this year precisely in the hottest season, July, does not deter Sadat from exercising to keep up his physical condition.

"But I find jogging really rather exaggerated. During the negotiations at Camp David President Carter asked me repeatedly to run with him, but a quick walk is enough for me. Why do I do it? I am convinced that a man cannot think if his body is not fit. God put us on this earth to be constructive. In order to achieve this the Almighty gave us three instruments: the soul, the mind and the body. You must find an ideal balance among these three elements in order to be efficient. The best way to nourish the soul? With faith, with religion. Faith brings answers in dark moments, when you are sure there is no way out . . . A well-nourished soul, if I may put it that way, saves mankind from doubt. And then the mind. In contrast to you Christians or the Jews, we have no prophets who performed miracles, as

Christ or Moses are supposed to have done. For us there is but one Godly miracle: the mind. The food for the mind is what the Persians call 'tavahona', knowledge. Yes, I speak Persian . . . This knowledge is not mystical, but concrete, empirical. Man must train his mind, just like his body, so that it doesn't become lazy. Only by finding a balance between the three God-given elements can you become a significant human being, a creative thinker . . ."

Is this also a condition for attaining power?

"Yes, of course, though you must have talent as well. You must be able to see things in a wider perspective, to comprehend how things are interconnected. You need not be a scholar, but you must be a rational being with logical insight. But the most important thing is God's will. He is the one who ultimately determines who is to receive earthly, and therefore transient, power."

Although he neither eats nor drinks nor smokes from sunup till sundown, as prescribed by the Koran during Ramadan, he still maintains a quick pace.

"I do not feel ill during the days of fasting. On the contrary. During Ramadan my mind becomes very clear, I feel almost *high*. I enjoy it because I notice that I can think more clearly than at other times. Now that it occurs to me, the most important decisions in my life have been made during Ramadan. That cannot be a coincidence. When I fast, I am closer to God, I understand better what He wants, what He expects from me. Then I see the Light and know which path I must take in order to fulfill my mission. A mission, does that sound strange? Doesn't everyone have a mission?"

Like two lions in a cage, we pace back and forth over the tiled path. In the distance the Koran is being read aloud in a mosque, where loudspeakers send the holy words into space. With a nonchalant gesture Sadat throws the used tissues into the bushes behind him. A servant will pick them up later. We speak of vocation: whether it isn't arrogant to think that Anwar Sadat was specially chosen by God for a higher mission . . .

"That has nothing to do with arrogance. I know, I simply feel, that God has given me a task to fulfill. In order to discover that, you must first have the opportunity to get to know yourself, your soul. My biography is called *In Search of Identity*, but what I really mean by that is: in search of my own identity. I found it in a strange place: in cell 54, where I was kept in isolation after being suspected of conspiring to murder the politician Osman. I sat there in the dark, no books, no newspapers, no radio. Alone. I had only myself to fall back on or I would break down. God helped me to discover my true self. Once I had discovered that, I knew that I had to devote my life to peace. That is what I have always worked towards, and so I was surprised that outsiders regarded my journey to Jerusalem in 1977 as a surprise. It was a logical consequence of my way of thinking."

Having had nothing to drink all day, Sadat has difficulty speaking and looks at me half in earnest, half in jest, when he says that he makes a point of not giving interviews during Ramadan. But this is not an interview – rather a conversation between two friends about friendship, love and death. Only a man who no longer needs to create a distance between himself and others in order to lend credibility to his authority can speak this way.

The *Rais*, as the Egyptians call their president, stops for a moment at the gate at the end of the path and chats with an old neighbour, who remains seated on his donkey. The man still lives next to the house where Sadat was born, on the other side of the village.

"We lived in the poorest neighbourhood of Mit Abu el Kom. I was an ordinary farmer's son who just managed to escape dying of hunger, but that was all. And yet I have the best memories of this village, where I feel at home among my people. They are simple but civilized, a natural consequence of their rich history of seven thousand years . . ."

He confesses that he wants to spend his old age here. When that will be, Sadat does not want to predict. Is he threatened in his position in anyway?

"How can I say? Whether I stay on or not depends on the will of God and on that of my people. It is no one's concern when I myself decide to leave office. When I feel that I have reached my peak as a creative human being, I will go, whether my people wish it or not." The Rais does not notice the contradiction. He does not seem to doubt for one second who will ultimately determine his future. Sadat alone will.

Self-confidence is the last thing Anwar Sadat lacks. His belief in God and in himself are weapons no non-believer can fight.

"Without faith you might just as well commit suicide . . . ," he says. But now he is not really speaking, he is shouting, as if he were addressing a crowd. A mass of people whom he must convince, whose concentration he demands. The corpulent bodyguard walking behind us with a pistol stuck ostentatiously in his belt is used to this. He reacts only to the subtle gestures addressed to him, as when the president notices that one of the spigots in the garden is leaking and orders the gardener to be called. The spigot is repaired instantly. For a moment his authoritarian streak surfaces, that characteristic which has led so many critics to compare Sadat with a Pharaoh. The people do indeed worship him like a Pharaoh, although Sadat views himself more as a trinity: the fellah, or farmer, in his gallabiah; the pasha or citizen in his proper pinstripe suit; the soldier in his marshal's uniform. Tradition, the modern West and the leader, all in one. Does he consciously cultivate the people's worship?

"Critics sometimes say that I prefer wearing a uniform, because most of the portraits throughout the country show me that way. I can do nothing about that. The ministry decided that that is what I look best in! . . . Perhaps a uniform is a sign of power. I don't know, but I am no dictator. . . . Besides, I only wear a uniform on very special occasions, such as a national holiday or a military parade. And, unfortunately, in wartime. . . . It may be true that the people look up to me. Egypt is not unique in that respect, you know. It is that way in every country where people want to free themselves from the yoke of poverty. The Egyptians need a leader, someone they can trust. Once that trust has been established, no one can destroy it. Look at Nasser. The people adored him, even after the humiliating defeat by Israel in 1967, even after it had become clear that he was threatening to cause the country's downfall. That blind trust came out very clearly during Nasser's funeral, when five million people poured into the streets to pay him their last respects."

The conversation turns naturally to Nasser, a subject that divides opinion in Egypt even now. Sadat has an ambivalent attitude towards the politician whom he served for eighteen years without fully agreeing with his policies. "Nasser remained my friend. That is the answer. Once a friend, always a friend . . ." Sadat would often repeat this maxim.

In a moment of stillness Sadat picks up a bunch of grapes and offers them to me. After praising the quality of the fruit this nature lover extols the abundant harvest.

"The lemons are brought up before they are ripe. A merchant comes to assess the value of the crop, then he makes an offer and sends his people to protect the orchard from thieves."

As if anything could be stolen here. The house and its related buildings are guarded like a fortress by special presidential guards with blue berets and by security officers

9

who keep an eye on the president day and night. You can't get into a car without stumbling over machine guns, everywhere there are pistols in holsters hanging nonchalantly over the back of a chair or sticking out of trouser pockets. The peacemaker, like all great leaders, is under constant threat. From everyone and from no one, which is precisely what makes the guards so nervous.

Just to enter the front garden you need a special pass, and all your belongings are examined; even confidants may be potential enemies and it is noticeable that close associates who have been with Sadat for more than ten years are frisked. But you never get the feeling that Sadat is afraid of death or worried about an attempt on his life. His adventurous history as a freedom fighter and his faith contribute to his fearlessness.

For the nth time in our stroll we make an about-face. Sadat explains that he is preparing for the coming visits to the United States and Great Britain. Does he ever feel like taking revenge on his former British enemies?

"No, Egyptians are a forgiving people. I fought like a lion against the British, but I respect them nevertheless. Let me repeat: I only distrust people who do not keep their word. That has nothing to do with nationality or even with political persuasion. Egypt has no need of anyone or anything and therefore does not have to hold on to its friends under false pretences. Just look at the Russians, I threw them out because it became apparent that they were bringing my country to the brink of bankruptcy. But there are also Americans with whom I did not feel comfortable, whom I did not really trust. On occasion the United States has been more intractable than the Soviet Union. Under Johnson and Dulles, for example. They were imperialists.... After the Vietnam war the United States was crippled, and I was very afraid because I thought that they would be unable to salvage their sullied image. The Vietnam complex had such a paralyzing effect that the Russians were able to do as they pleased, in the Middle East and elsewhere. The situation was so serious that America itself was threatened. But Ronald Reagan's America is the one from before Vietnam. Self-assured and energetic. It is still too early to know how this will benefit us, but I am glad that the Americans have come out of their isolation. President Carter did not know how to deal with this isolation either. And now that we are talking about him: what kind of country is it that drops a man like Carter like a hot brick? You can't simply forget about an honest politician, religious and sincere, who did not only the Middle East but also the prestige of the United States a great service by his tremendous contribution to the realization of the Camp David agreements. Without him, without America, there would have been no peace at all in this area...."

He has finished his walk. His masseur, Zenhom, stands ready to rub the Rais down after he has spent yet another fifteen minutes on an exercise bicycle. After this massage, a daily ritual, Sadat lies flat on his back for an hour to meditate.

"I need a lot of time to think about my people, to philosophize about my policy. I do that at home. I never leave the office later than about five o'clock. By then I have spoken with enough other people, then I need to be alone."

During Ramadan Sadat only works after nine in the evening, after dinner. Until two or three in the morning he reads and writes or receives ministers and advisers. During the day the prayers and the reading of the Koran interrupt government activity.

After his meditation, Sadat withdraws into his bedroom, where he sits crosslegged in front of two cushions piled one on top of the other and reads aloud from a gilded Koran. On the book he places a microphone, which is connected to a tape recorder. Sitting there in his pyjama-like jacket, he looks as if he were preparing a sermon. Does he feel that his task as president is not only political but also spiritual?

"If you are speaking of religious activities, no. I am not a preacher but a political leader in the true sense of the word. That means that I bear certain responsibilities, but not that I am superior to others. Islam makes no distinction between people, at the most it requires that the political leader guarantee a correct interpretation of the religion. He must ensure that his people live according to the laws of Islam." The world has seen the excesses to which this can lead in a country such as Iran.

"Yes, yes, alas. I have protested more than once against what is happening there. Khomeini has turned things back to front. He is a spiritual leader with political delusions of grandeur. A kind of prophet who thinks he can play at being God . . . Even the true prophets were people with faults, not angels. But Khomeini thinks he is elevated above everyone and everything. What he is doing in the name of Islam is a disgrace to all Muslims. What he practises is not religion, but Khomeinism! Islam is not hate, or blood, or revenge . . . . But to get back to the tapes: I would like to leave my children and grandchildren a Koran read aloud by me personally, as moral support. A spoken book, as it were . . ."

Sadat continues his reading of the Koran with great concentration, drowning out the hum of the tape recorder. He wears reading glasses, which make him look older; and he is himself as much a combination of modernism and tradition as the tape recorder and the holy book.

In the corner of the bedroom stands a bed with many cushions, where he sleeps between lace sheets. There are no books, but a television set is at hand. Anwar Sadat is addicted to everything having to do with movies, and has even installed video equipment in his planes. When he has time, what he prefers to do after dinner is watch 16 mm films projected on a large screen that accompanies him everywhere. Here too, in Mit Abu el Kom, it is set up in a room. He shares this mania with such American presidents as Jimmy Carter. Jasmine water is on the dressing table. In the hall leading to the dressing room, where Sadat's personal servant waits discreetly, is the trusty exercise bicycle.

Anwar Sadat loves simplicity. No pretentious furniture, no art objects. His residences in Aswan, Cairo, Mit Abu el Kom, Ismaelia and Maamourah near Alexandria resemble one another in their efficiency and asceticism.

On the balcony, Sadat, now clad in a white gallabiah, stretches out his arms and resembles figures in the Luxor tombs. There is something sovereign about him, which he himself probably does not even realize, as he speaks of his country. He is not prepared to see how relative the accomplishments of Egyptian society are when he speaks of the tremendous progress and the far-reaching democracy that make Egypt virtually a Western country. It is thanks to the innate patience of his people that he is not confronted more often with the true economic and social problems. Naturally things are better than they were ten or eleven years ago, but objectively speaking, there is as yet no reason to be completely satisfied. Independence? Without the United States, Egypt is just as incapacitated as Israel. Democracy? Yes, compared to other countries in the Middle East, but not compared to the West, contrary to what Sadat is so fond of stating. His opinion of freedom of the press speaks volumes:

"Our constitution says that we must guarantee freedom of the press as part and parcel of democracy. I understand that but I don't really agree with it. Whether we like it or not, the newspapers and television provide the people with information every day, and for that reason they can be very dangerous instruments if they fall into the wrong hands. That is why I am against private ownership of the press. In the end, owners of newspapers and weekly magazines are totally dependent on the advertisers and can therefore be manipulated. They cannot be neutral or objective."

Sadat has reason enough to distrust the media. Not long ago a photograph which appeared in the international press showed him lying on the floor meditating. In a Libyan newspaper it was described as "Sadat, leader of Egypt, on the ground", and other hostile Arab leaders also used it to ridicule him. It is a telling sign of Sadat's self-confidence, in view of incidents of this kind, that we are allowed to walk about unhindered in his presence.

On the veranda, dinner is ready on a table that was laid hours before. The sun goes down while two of his daughters rise from a rocking chair and respectfully kiss his hand, and then his cheek. *Pater familias,* as he is the father of Egypt. Perhaps that is the best description of his relationship to the Egyptian people: head of the family. The television is on during this family dinner. Oleander, roasted meat, and his daughters' Western perfumes combine in a tropical mélange, made unreal by the noise of the TV and the gray glow it casts over the table.

After dinner, cars come driving into the garden: Sadat is going to visit two cousins who live at the other end of Mit Abu el Kom and have invited him over for tea. The cars take a longer route than necessary so as not to disappoint the local population – after all, it's not every day that the Rais is here – and on the way the cavalcade is cheered. Women utter shrill screams, a sort of gurgling yodel, meant as a sign of joy. In the very simple house of Sadat's relatives he is greeted like a prodigal son: he kisses and gets kissed and hugged. Doors and windows are filled to bursting with people, all of whom want to touch 'their' president.

With his cane between his legs he listens intently to the villagers, and from time to time sips tea from a glass. As protection in a writhing mass of people like this is practically impossible, the security guards watch helplessly.

The gathering does not last long. Sadat yearns again for the quiet of his room, for prayer. On the veranda he glances up at the moon, takes leave in a friendly but distracted fashion and disappears into the house to meditate until deep in the night. When we leave the grounds of the residence to drive back to the capital, the neighbours are still sitting out of doors having dinner. The air smells of horse manure, tahin, mangos and dust.

It is not until we leave Cairo for the second time the next day to drive through the Nile delta to Mit Abu el Kom that we notice that, all appearances to the contrary, Sadat's native village is not like the other settlements we pass. Of course the men all look the same in their none too clean gallabiahs or their short plusfours on their donkeys, which are carrying unidentifiable grass-like matter under the coercion of short, sharp blows of a stick. Nor do the half-blind fellahs, symbols of the unhygienic conditions along the Nile, and the pecking chickens on the roofs of the mud huts to the left of the main road differ much from such tableaux elsewhere. Here too children play with self-made 'cars' of wire: a steering wheel connected diagonally to a small wheel, with which they go tearing over the sandy paths, 'honking' wildly. But they do not beg, they do not shout "Baksheesh, baksheesh, mister." The Rais has forbidden it. And another, more important difference: a relatively large number of inhabitants of Mit Abu el Kom have 'real' houses of red brick, built at Sadat's own expense, as a number of signs announce. The profits from his autobiography are deposited in a special fund for the modernization of the village.

The security measures at the entrance to Sadat's grounds are still just as stringent. It gets too hot waiting in the garden, and for a while we occupy one of the guard's rooms. Nevertheless we are taken by surprise when we are admitted

12

to the tiled path again. He is wearing a different colour but otherwise the same gym suit. Is it thanks to the climate or to the Oriental mentality that Sadat has so much more time for himself than politicians in the West? After all, Egypt is a strategically important country with a great many ambitions in both foreign and domestic politics... Wouldn't the world look different if, for example, President Reagan or Chancellor Schmidt were to allow themselves more leisure for meditating, working out their problems? Or would that be impossible without a certain philosophy?

"I do not call that philosophy. In the West no one has time to devote to himself, the material pressure is too great. Presumably that cannot be changed, and so I understand that people live differently there. When I get the chance I do try to explain to my colleagues in Europe or the United States how I divide up my day and why. Politics and religion, for example, are closely interconnected here, and as a result there is automatically time for prayer, which is also a form of meditation. Chancellor Schmidt was especially interested in my philosophy. I explained to him the meaning of the Koran, how much this book resembles the Bible in some places. How clear it is that we are all brothers in love. And he, rational thinker that he is, understood it all. He stimulated me to write my book, in which I compare the three great religions, among other things..." The president never tires of talking about Schmidt, whom he calls either "Herr Kanzler" or "Herr Führer", the latter with a malicious grin, knowing very well what connotations this term still has. "It is just a word. You Europeans are so sensitive..." It's time for his massage again.

In the reception room of one of the annexes where the guards stay, the atmosphere is so tense you could cut it with a knife. The high officers – majors, colonels and brigadier-generals – are forced to sleep two and sometimes three to a room; some have to sleep on the floor. In pure frustration a major sends a chair flying through the room. Especially the chain smokers are having a hard time at Ramadan. After sunset, the first thing they reach for is a pack of cigarettes, and only then do they think of food.

Every year Sadat invites what he calls his 'poor relations' to a banquet. This always takes place during Ramadan and no members of the press are ever admitted. Sadat does not want to create the impression that he is making this gesture for the sake of publicity. Critics should be cured of their prejudices by now, though: after all, a president with poor relations is living proof that there is little or no corruption in Egypt.

Some hundred dressed-up men and women, young fathers, bent grandmothers and chirping children have been waiting for two hours on the blue and yellow benches lining the walls of the reception room. You do not arrive late for an appointment with the Rais, and you can usefully spend your waiting time looking at the photographs of your uncle, cousin or second cousin that cover all the walls. Two large fans hanging from the ceiling make a pretence of producing fresh air, though in fact they are only stirring clammy air.

Outside, among the bushes and the shorn grass alongside the house, a yards-long table that the servants have been working on all afternoon has been set up; here all the guests can be seated. They have come from near and far; how they got here is a mystery, for there are no cars outside the gate. Today, as every day, Radio Cairo announces the exact moment when the sun sinks below the horizon and everyone can act normal again. While the relatives start devouring their food hungrily after sixteen hours of fasting, Sadat briefly postpones breaking his fast; he kneels in front of the table, touches his forehead to the ground and prays in the direction of Mecca for the umpteenth time today, controlled and concentrated. A dark spot on his bald forehead, almost a growth, is proof of his zeal.

Sadat eats little. He drinks water and keeps this gathering as short as others which will take place during the period of fasting. He sits in a rocking chair at the head of the table, nodding beneficently at the hungry guests. His dishes and cutlery are different from those of the guests: a crystal goblet instead of an ordinary glass, dark blue plates with gold edging. And his napkin is folded not in the shape of an ordinary triangle but rather into a mitre. We eat with the servants. Eggplant, rice, tahin, lettuce, cucumbers, mutton ragout, watermelon and sickly sweet cake. There are no fewer than three glasses next to our plate: one with brown fig juice and fruit, another contains a milky brew and the third water. We stick to Pepsi.

After dinner Sadat changes out of his gallabiah into an elegant black silk suit to receive the Spanish ambassador, who has requested an audience. As at every official occasion, however short or unimportant, the Egyptian television is present to broadcast the Rais' every activity. There is a special two-man team who follow Sadat everywhere and pop up at the most unexpected moments.

After the diplomat has paid his respects, prayers are held once again. Proudly the president shows how he can determine the precise direction of Mecca, after having fetched a watch from his night-table: "A Swiss invention! Look, everything is written on it in Arabic.... With the help of one of the hands and a disc with all the important cities of the world on it, I can determine the direction of Mecca. I had a bit of difficulty at Camp David, which wasn't on the watch, but who knows, maybe by the time the watch is produced again Camp David will have been promoted to the rank of important places...." He laughs and explains that he does not need the watch here and that it always shows 'foreign' time, whatever that may mean.

Ramadan has been going on for three weeks by the time the Sudanese president visits Alexandria, a favourite refuge when it gets too hot in Khartoum. Sadat regards Sudan as an ally that deserves Egypt's help and gets it, even though there might be just a tiny bit of self-interest involved. Evil tongues say that Sudan is nothing more than an Egyptian protectorate, but Sadat himself views President Numeiry as an 'ally' with whom he lives together on the Nile. Sadat moves to the summer residence in Maamourah near Alexandria, on the coast, where he can entertain his guest and offer him a piece of Egyptian land to establish a tax-free zone in order to boost the Sudanese economy. Here, too, are beautifully kept gardens, where pink and white predominate. A tennis court and a playground do no disrupt the natural environment so much as the security measures along the beach do: barbed wire barricades extend far into the water. Soldiers without even a lean-to or a tent to shelter them from the burning sun keep watch behind sandbags. On closer inspection Maamourah is a hermetically sealed camp, with a gigantic concrete building for the President and roomy quarters for the security officers who live here with their families.

To reach the Rais' secretariat we pass three or four guardposts; the guards continue to be suspicious, no matter how often we visit Maamourah. Neither special passes nor our amiability help to speed up the admission procedure, which takes longer every day. Patience is a virtue with which the Egyptians are more richly endowed than we are, but the incessant waiting forces us to learn it. Hours on end we spend waiting in clammy waiting rooms, where belly dancers exhibit their talents on a poorly tuned television set.

Getting to the secretariat, which still lies outside the president's 'real' garden, is a big step in the right direction. Feeling hopeful, we relax in wicker chairs or go for a walk along the beach, not knowing whether there might be landmines buried there. The masseur Zenhom presses 120 kilos as if they were a bag of feathers: he has five black belts in judo, a small-caliber pistol in his sport trousers and the most attractive face of all the men in Sadat's entourage. Zenhom keeps his weights in the hangar at the far end of the beach, next to an American landing craft and broken-down outboard motors awaiting repair. After nearly four hours of waiting, a guard brings us the all too familiar message: NO WALK TODAY. That means that we will not be allowed to meet Sadat. All our waiting was for nothing.

Two days later we are in luck. The Rais, so open during conversations but so closed as soon as they are over, wants to see us. We stand for a moment next to a cage with two chimpanzees, an official gift from an African country, and get moving the minute the guard shouts WALK NOW. Sadat's wife, Jehan, is joining us today. In her blue gym suit and red baseball cap she looks quite Western, and her freckles betray the English blood on her mother's side. She keeps up a quick pace, subtly adding her remarks to those of her husband. We speak of love.

"If I can do it, why can't others? I mean make a pact with your heart. Jealousy and hatred and other lowly instincts must make way for understanding. Only love can bring about miracles. Of course love is closely bound up with faith, with religion, if only you open your eyes to to it. In neighbouring countries where religion is just as important as in ours, you sometimes doubt the leaders' insight. In Iran, Libya, but in Israel too. And then I am speaking of the hawks. I sometimes wonder whether they will ever learn anything from Jerusalem and Camp David. Many Israelis continue to distrust the outside world, and distrust is not a good basis for love...."

After the first couple of meetings we wonder whether it is because of Ramadan fasting that Sadat propounds such a simple view of the world. Is he naive? Or are we at fault, no longer accustomed to honest opinions that go straight to the heart of the matter?

"In prison and on the battlefield you come to know yourself," he writes in his autobiography. Does everything become simple then? Or has he only reached the peak of his insight after all these years at the top? For no matter how naive Sadat may sound when you speak to him in private, you cannot ignore his past. It reveals him as a natural politician, a cunning fox, who knew just what concessions to make at just the right moment, who picked the right friends and took decisions which made a simple farmer's boy president in a country where the American dream is still a dream. You couldn't really call Anwar Sadat a wolf in sheep's clothing either, though, for he is too convincing, he has too much integrity. But he is like a chameleon, adapting quickly to circumstances, sensitive to ways of manipulating crowds or his guests and hosts. The Sadat we meet during a walk or at home is not Sadat, the Head of State.

His dialogue with himself and with his intimate surroundings brings him such peace of mind that he never really feels the need of a vacation. Sadat also reads less than he used to, particularly foreign literature, although he reads German and especially English fluently. His family – daughters and sons-in-law, grandchildren – is clearly a source of earthly happiness. He has a lot of time for them, is proud of the fact that the women – including his own wife – are able to lead respectable and active lives of their own, thanks to his liberal attitudes.

"It is not easy," says Jehan Sadat, "to play an independent role in a conservative country. Many men still regard staying at home, raising the children and cooking as more honorable occupations than working. We women are not against tradition, but the whole world is changing, so we too must think of our emancipation. There are 34 women in our parliament, women in city councils, on boards of directors of companies. By Muslim standards that is a real revolution, although the Koran never discriminated against women. The men did that themselves, and it has simply taken a long time for us to realize what our rights are. Women ask questions, are active partners in society, contribute to the country's development, its progress . . ."

Progress: an aspiration many a Muslim leader has stumbled over. We get onto the subject of Iran again, and we wonder whether there is not a threat of conflict between tradition and modernism, between Oriental values and Western challenges.

"There are fanatics everywhere, in Egypt too, who try to delude the people into thinking that development and prosperity will harm Islam and that they are contrary to the Koran. I do not believe that they will find any support in this civilized country. Religious extremists are not taken seriously here . . ." The attentive listener might catch an undertone of superiority, expressing perhaps not disdain for the non-Egyptians in the Middle East but certainly the awareness of being different from the 'others'. In any case it is not surprising that the Arab brethren have difficulty with this man, who would have had enemies even without Camp David. He is not fundamentally averse to the Arab world, though, which he needs more than he wants to admit. Saudi Arabia's increasing sympathy for Sadat's peace strategy in the Middle East, unofficial though it may be, provides important support for the Rais, for he continues to need successes, both political and economic. In contrast to King Hussein of Jordan, for example, he has no section of the population that will support him come what may. He can be as sure as he wants of the support of his people, but without bread and circuses not even Sadat can succeed. As long as he keeps the peace and manages to increase Egypt's prestige through diplomatic manoeuvres he can rest assured of foreign investment. But more than ever before, he is dependent on his neighbors' goodwill for international success, and perhaps it is time to abandon the standpoint that the Arab brethren must come to him and not vice versa.

But it is not in Sadat's nature to ask favours. Even if he needs help from the Americans he'll manage to turn things around so that they will be the ones to have offered the help. Libya, a neighboring country, has been bothering Sadat for a long time, because of the "adventurous" spirit of Colonel Gaddafi whom Sadat cannot bear. But he prefers to undertake no direct action against Gaddafi for fear of causing even more tension in the delicate Middle East situation. Before visiting the United States he said that he would explain to America that Russian influence in the Middle East, which is channelled partly through the 'terrorists' protector' Gaddafi, cannot be tolerated; that it is time for Reagan to take a stand, as Gaddafi has been getting on his nerves for a long time, too . . . Sadat in the role of adviser in the great game between East and West. . . . With this strategy he kills two birds with one stone: it improves his standing with America, which has promised him even more financial and military aid, as well as in his own country, where he is the diplomat and angel of peace.

The fall of the monarchy in Egypt is commemorated that evening in an open-air theatre in Alexandria. On July 26, 1952, three days after the revolution which Nasser together with Anwar Sadat helped to bring about, King Farouk was forced into exile. President Numeiry is present, and the united northern forces offer him a silver sword. Sadat receives a blazon engraved with his memorable words of twenty-nine years ago: "On Egyptian soil there is no will but that of the Egyptians."

We are entertained by acrobats – most of them children – an orchestra, a terrible band and a pathetic diva in a peach-colored dress reading a poem she wrote herself. The evening drags on and on, as do most official occasions, which are apparently only taken seriously if they last at least four hours. Sadat looks a bit thinner. He is not unaffected by the fasting.

With sirens wailing, the cavalcade of cars and limousines drives to the airport the next day, where President Sadat is taking leave of his guests from Sudan. The procession, which passes crowds of cheering people, includes a metallic blue American station wagon: the mobile emergency operating room. This time the Heads of State sit behind bulletproof glass instead of in the open Lincoln with running boards, which seems to have been included in the procession to no purpose. There is a guard of honor, a red carpet. Kisses are exchanged and Numeiry flies away. The Rais leaves for Cairo with his wife on board a Mystère jet. We were to travel with him, but are unexpectedly pushed into a gigantic C-130, an Air Force transport plane. Before we know what is happening we find ourselves in a parody of a cabin in a passenger plane, with boarded windows, so that we do not know whether we are flying above land or water and are terrified at landing. Someone is airsick, and the ultimate irony is the movie shown on a video screen, *Those Magnificent Men in Their Flying Machines*. Nobody understands the words, but it doesn't matter, as everyone on board has already seen the movie. When we arrive we discover that Sadat has already left for the grave of Shah Reza Pahlavi, the purpose of this expedition. In the El Rifaay mosque he prays, together with the family of the emperor of Iran, who died a year ago in Cairo, in memory of this "friend who was repudiated by the entire world."

"They had no more use for him, that is what they said, as if the Shah were an object. Everyone left him to his fate, but by showing him the hospitality he deserved, the Egyptians have shown what friendship is, what moral values mean. Unlike others we have inner civilization, and we let spiritual interests prevail over material ones."

From Cairo we proceed with planes and helicopters to Damanrou, where Sadat visits a sick friend. The main thing you remember after a couple of days with Sadat is this: the president not only *seems* to hover between heaven and earth, he actually *does*. Out of one plane, into the next, out of one helicopter, into the other. And always on the double. Before you know it, he has disappeared again. For all the simplicity and asceticism of his personal life, everything to do with his travelling and official ceremony is not only elaborate but enormously expensive.

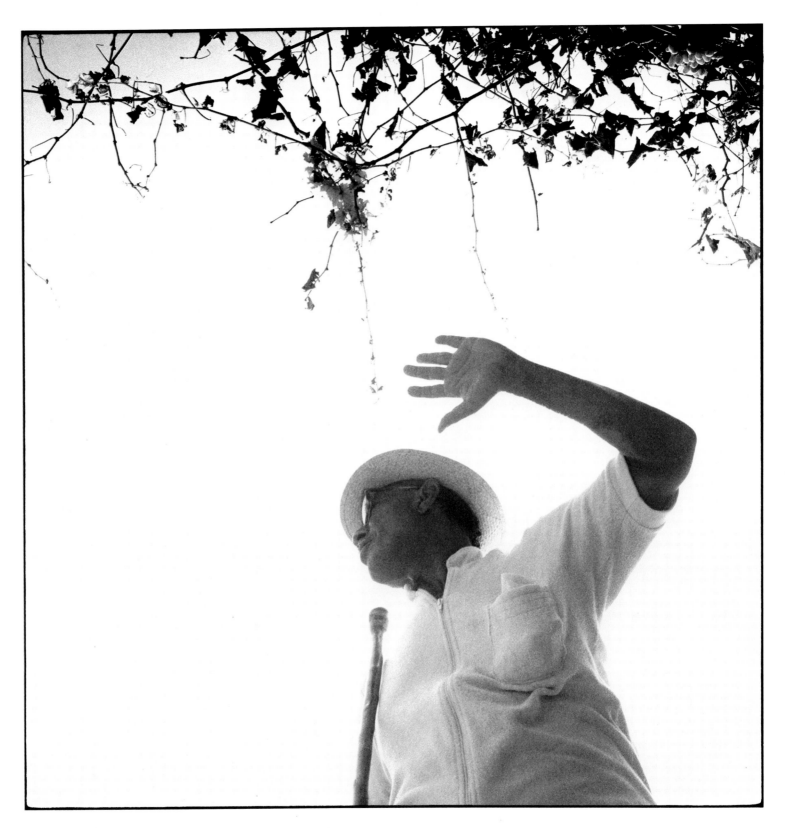

In the garden . . .

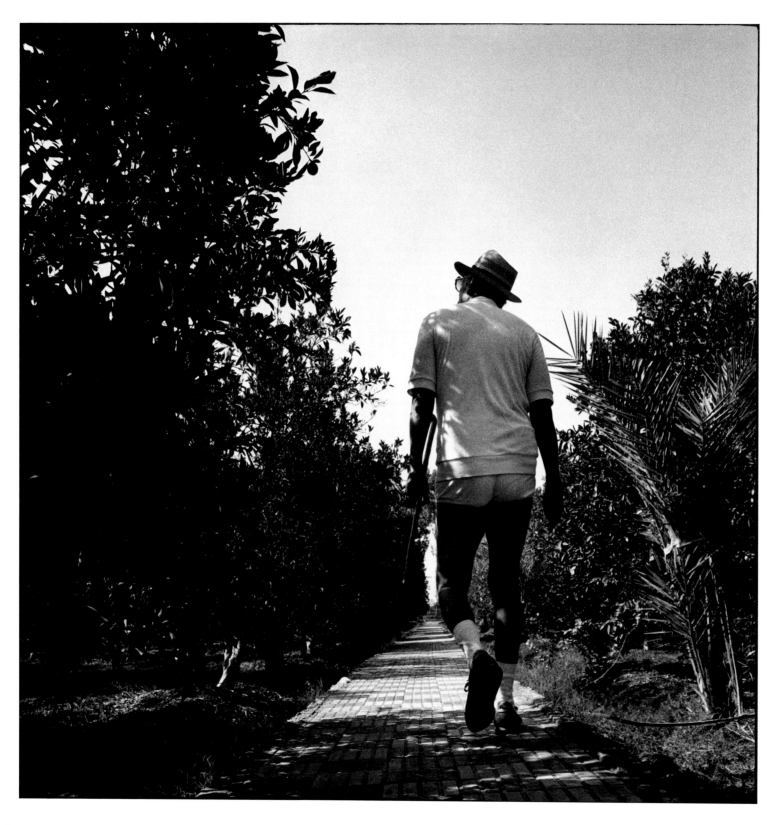

. . . of his house . . .

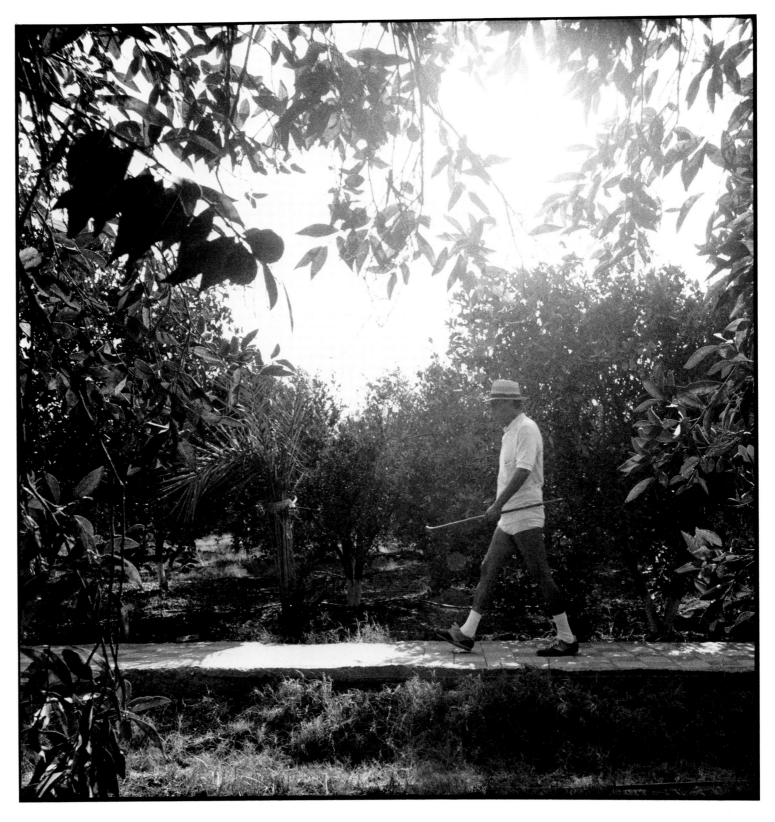

. . . at Mit Abu el Kom

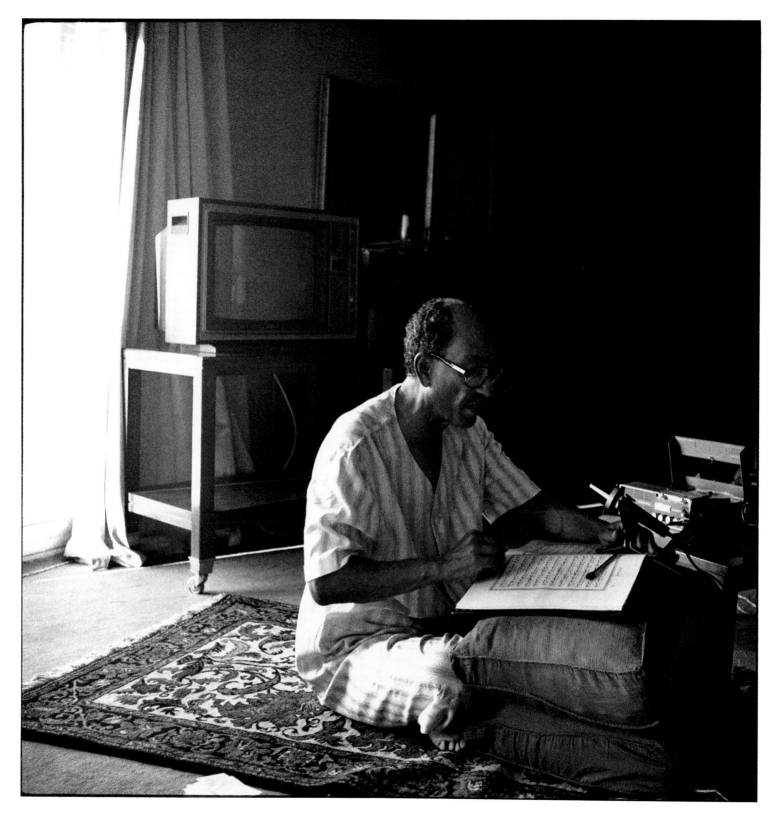

Reading the Koran

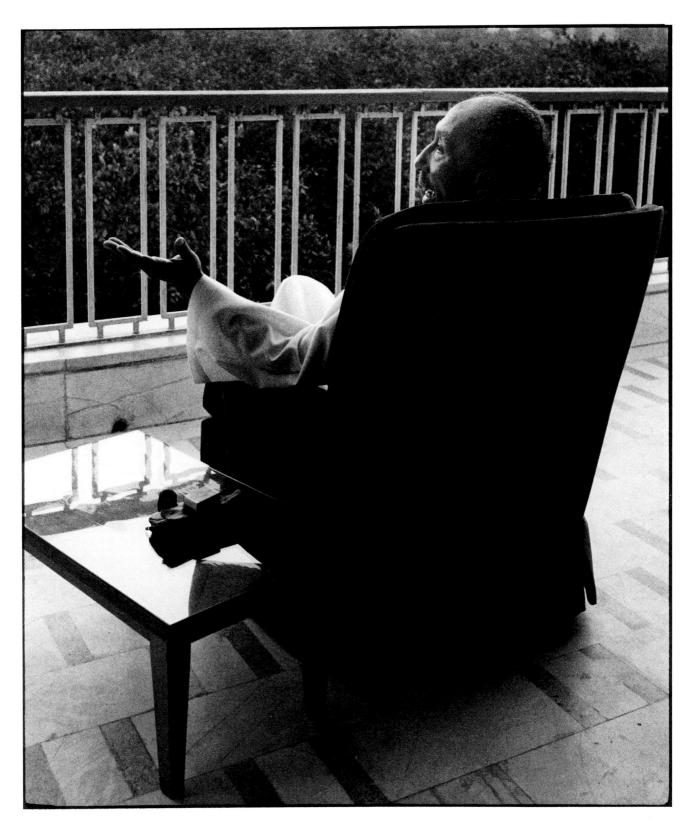

On the veranda

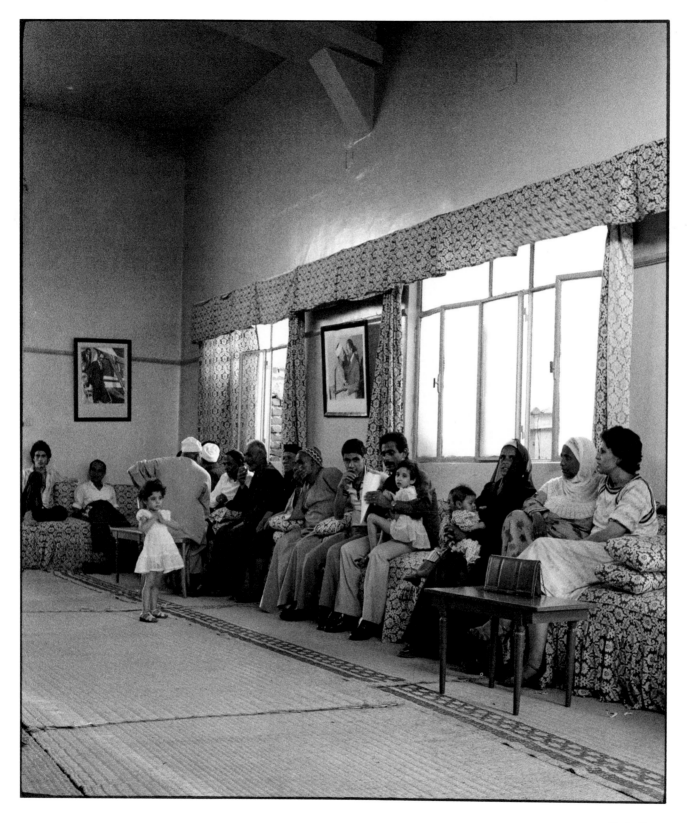

Relations

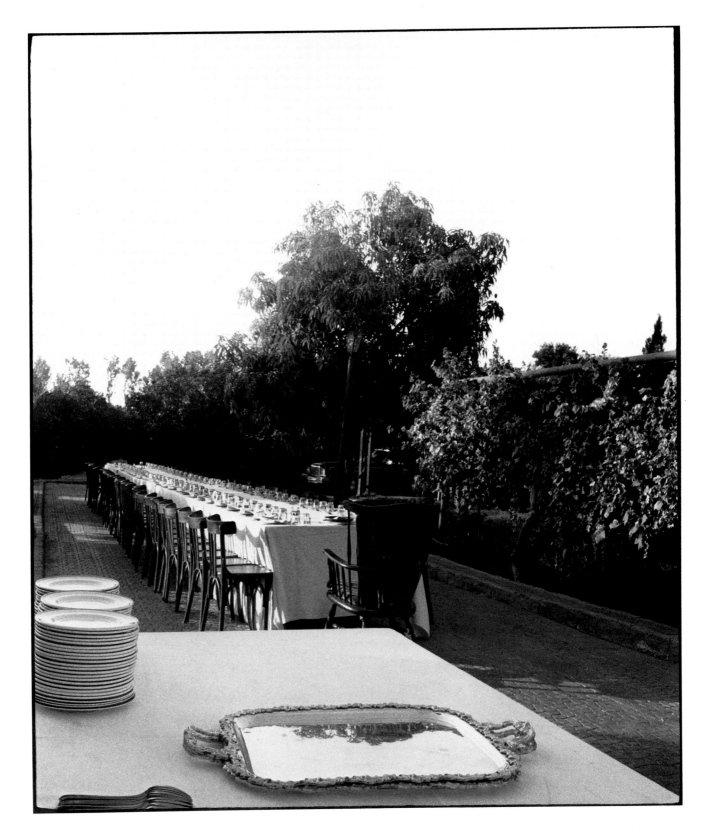

The table

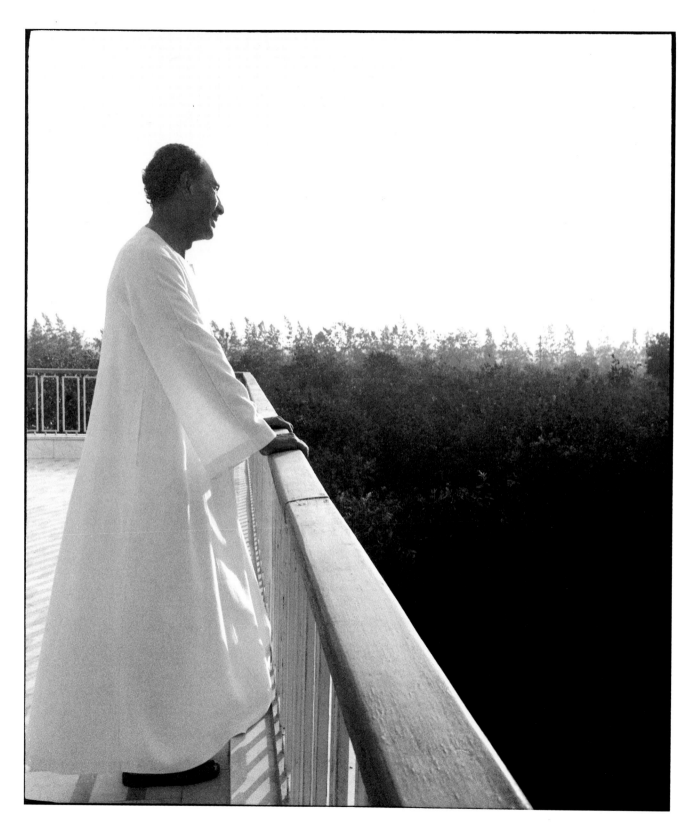

Gallabiya – the traditional dress of the *fellahin*

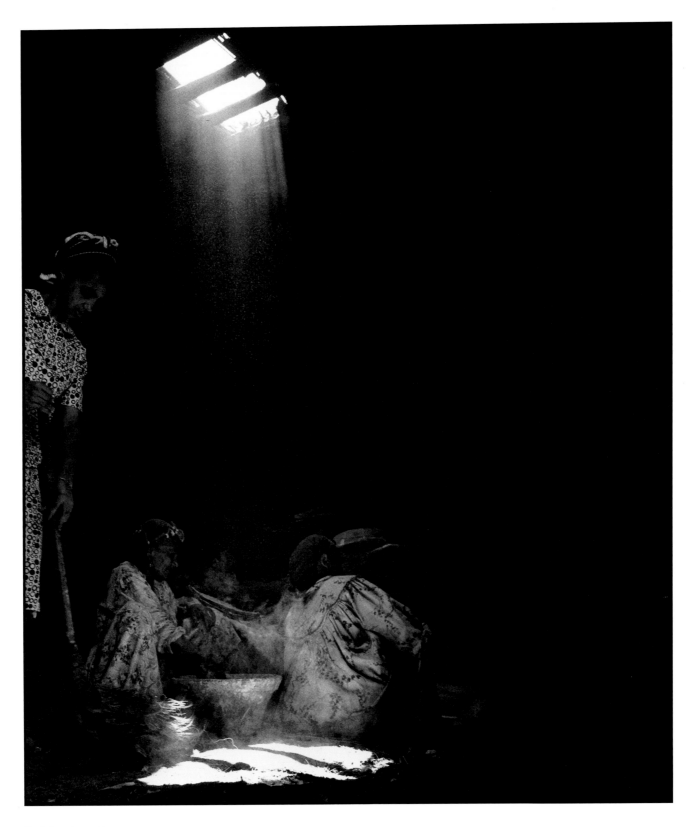

Baking bread

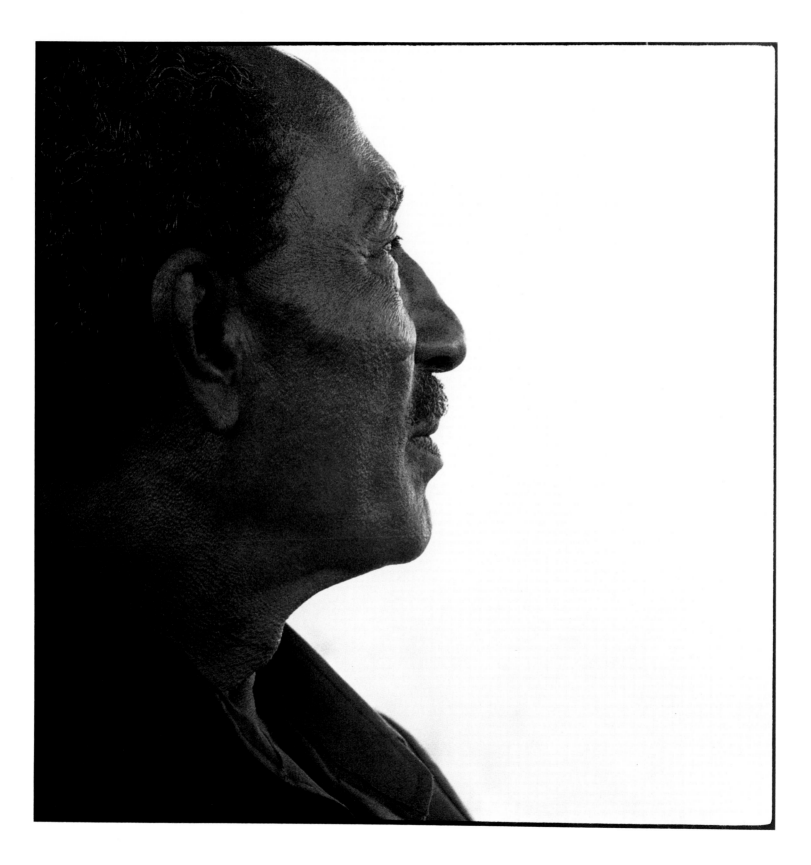

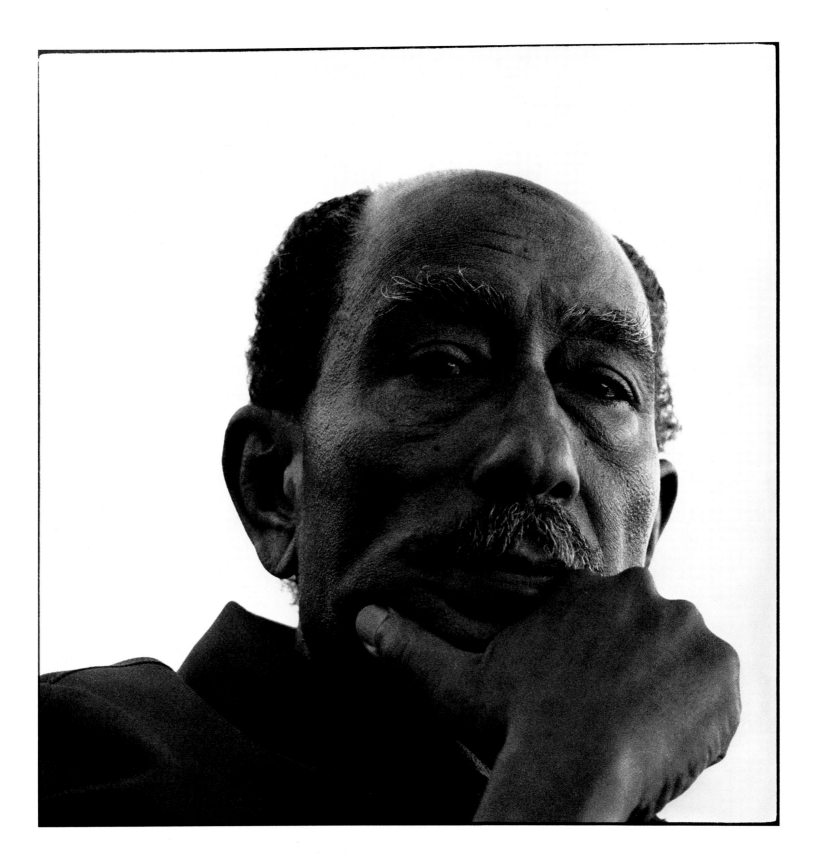

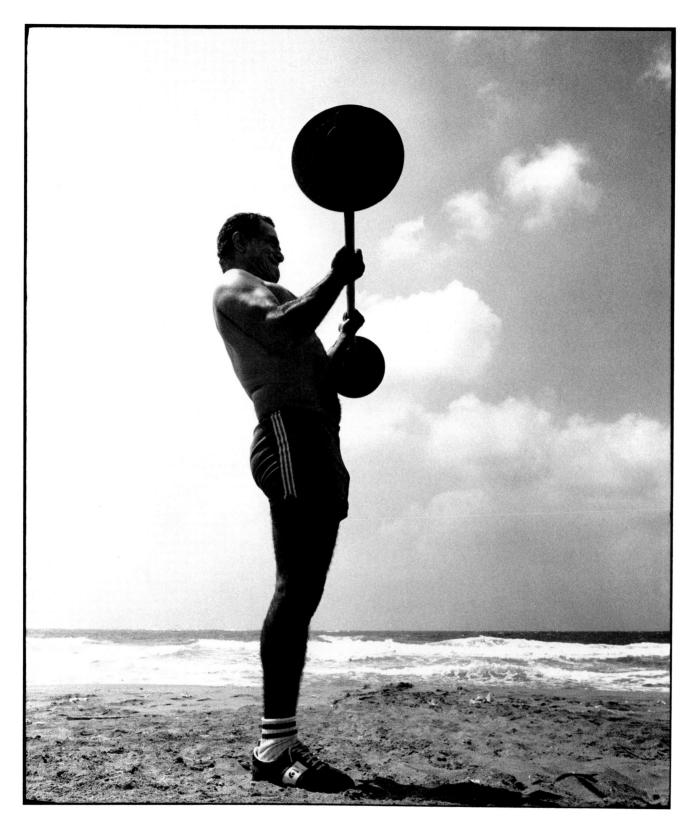

The masseur Zenhom

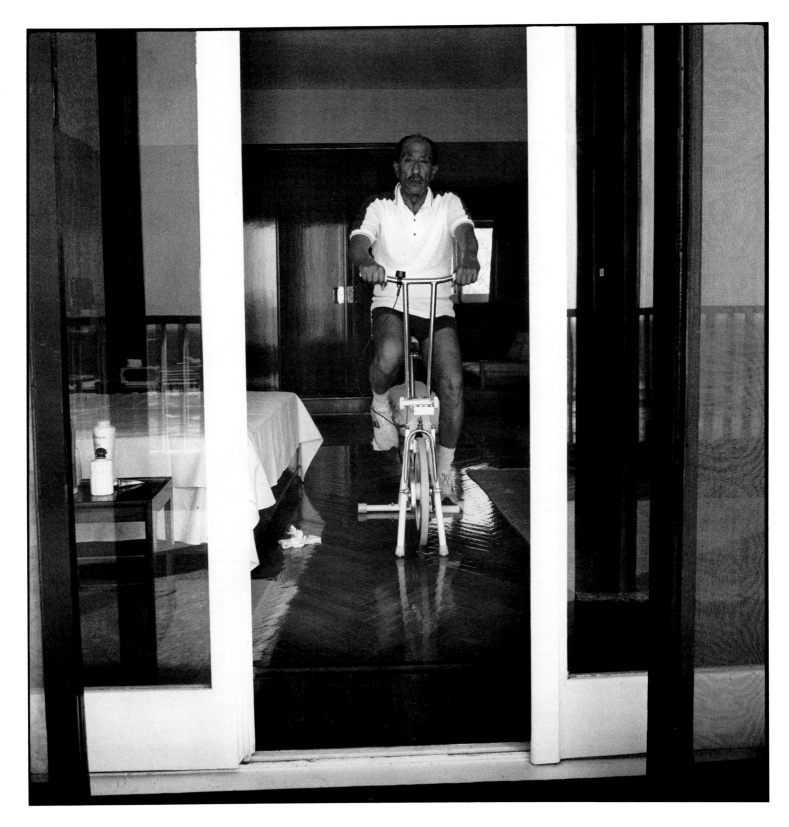

Training

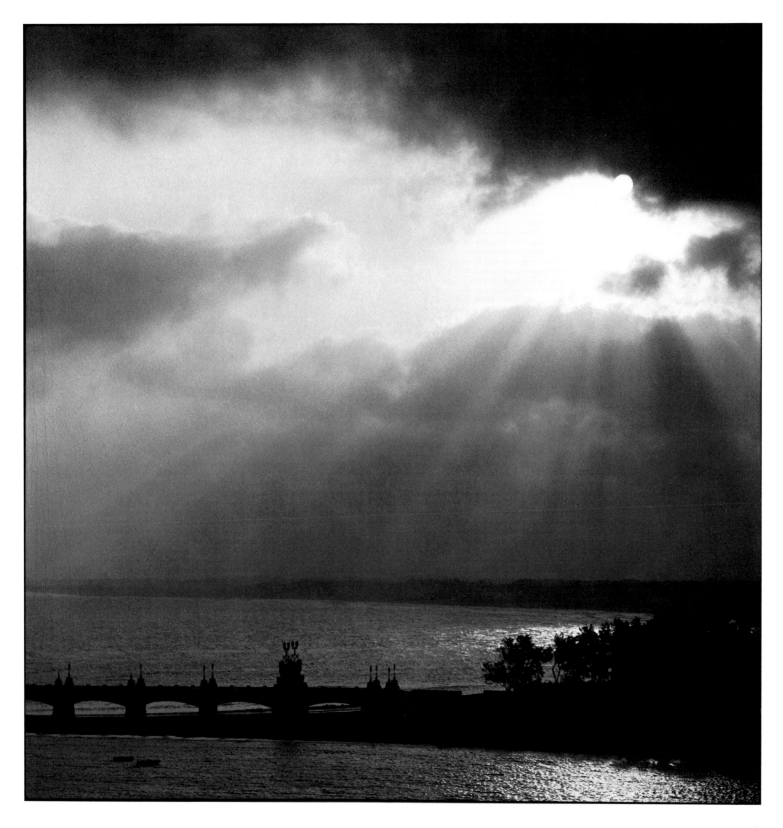

The coast at Maamourah

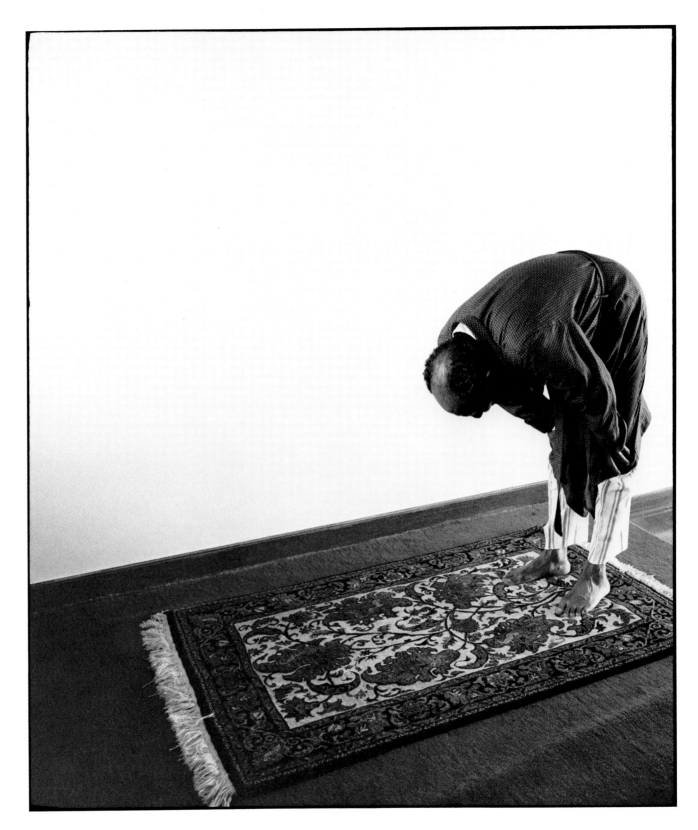

Prayer

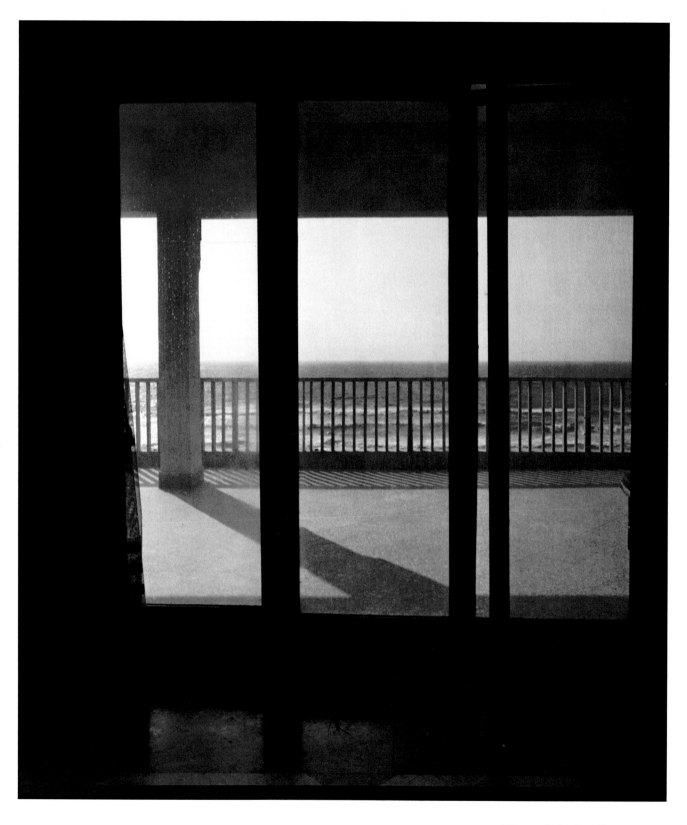

View of the Mediterranean

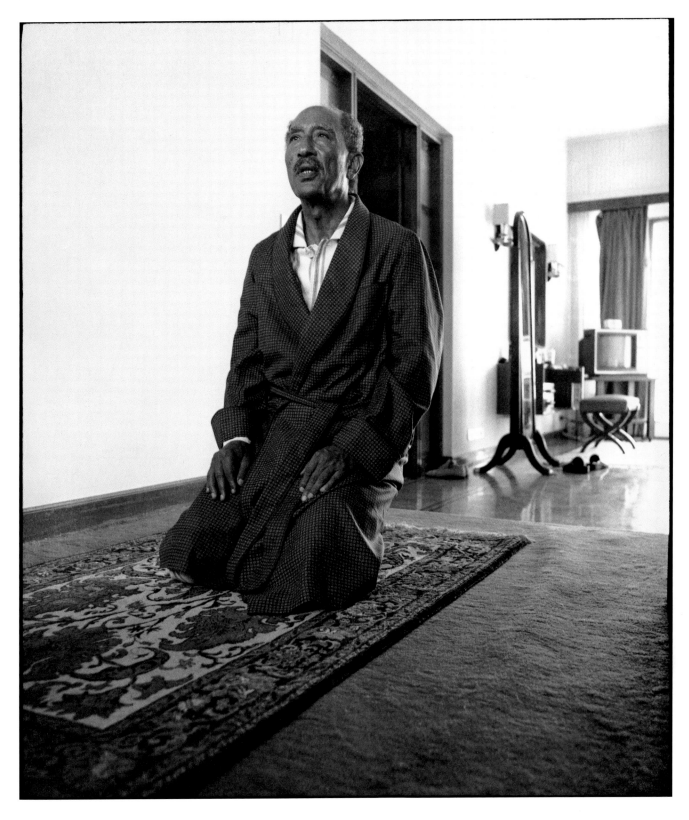

Prayer

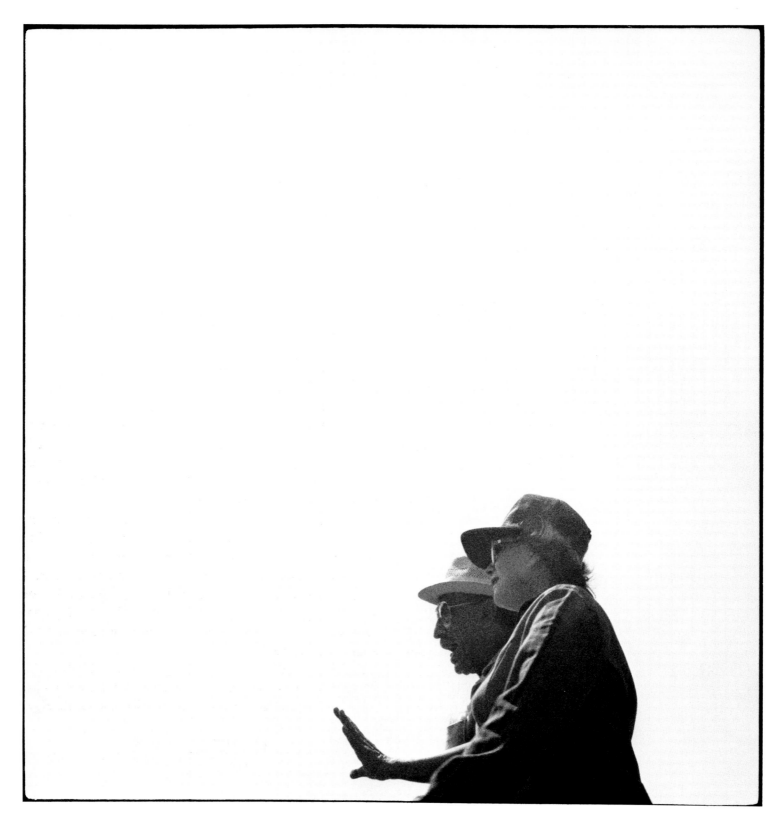

With his wife Jehan

II The Sinai

"The Sinai is for the Egyptians and for them alone. No one else has any business here." At last Sadat can justifiably speak of *his* Sinai: 80 per cent of the land captured by the Israelis is now back in Egyptian hands. "The Arab world criticized me severely. I was supposedly acting in my own interest, striving only towards a separate peace with Israel. The Arab brothers have tried to isolate me, but they have failed. Who is isolated? They. For it has been proven that my peace initiative is the only way to bring calm to the Middle East.

"Thanks to my first step, back there in Jerusalem, we got the Sinai back. Now we have oil and other natural resources. I thank God for this oil, which can make us independent . . .

"Now that we Egyptians live in peace with Israel, others must do the same. I will continue to fight for the Palestinians' right to self-determination, but they will have to take the initiative themselves. As everyone knows, the Palestinian problem will have to be solved before there can be true peace in this part of the world. Without Egypt, appointed by history as the leader of the Arab world, nothing can be achieved . . . The other countries are so divided amongst themselves that they cannot show their strength, cannot develop common tactics . . ."

An indestructible faith in his own ability, in his country's position, are really the hallmark of all the discussions about the Middle East situation. He sits on a small bench in front of one of the ten pastel-coloured houses in the Holy Valley, where he had a special camp built after the transfer of this part of the Sinai. This spot, at the base of the famous Greek Orthodox Saint Catherine monastery, does indeed breath peace and quite. It is at the base also of Mount Sinai, where Moses received the Ten Commandments.

"The mother of the Arab world is Egyptian, did you know that? We are the descendants of Abraham, just like the Jews. The father of the Jews is Israel, that of the Muslims Ishmael. They are both sons of Abraham, but had different mothers. The mother of Israel was Sarah, that of Ishmael Haggar, an Egyptian! Jews and Muslims are brothers who speak a different language but who are destined to find one another."

The sinking sun glows orange red on the dry flanks of the hills. Sadat says that he can barely control his emotions on this holy spot, a source not only of wisdom, but also of great strife. Now that the Sinai has changed hands, he wants to come here every year towards the end of Ramadan to pray, as he has done from the moment the helicopter brought him here from the minuscule airstrip at Sinai. He has kept his concentration, however; something that only professional believers are capable of in the West. He kneels on a carpet that he rolled out himself on the veranda of his primitive house. Apparently he prefers this to the simple mosque that has been built on the fenced-in terrain, where members of the delegation say their prayers.

Sadat has time for only one other pleasure besides prayer: his garden, with its melons and cucumbers, as well as the produce of the greenhouse, unreal elements in the middle of this endless desert, where you find green only around the scarce springs. The rest is sand, stone and hills as far as the eye can see. Suddenly Bedouins with camels appear out of nowhere, the same men who warmly greeted Sadat at the airport. They are the most important sheikhs of the southern Sinai, one of the two districts into which this desert has been divided. They have come to greet their leader: for the first time they notice that Cairo exists.

"When they were asked how the transfer of the Sinai affected them they answered: first there were the Israelis and now there are the Egyptians. So it doesn't really make any difference. When the British were here they neglected the Bedouins, kept them apart. The Israelis also ignored them, and for a long time even we did not know how to approach them. Last year I had all the sheikhs come to Cairo to tell them that the Sinai is theirs. That they are Egyptians. Until recently the Sinai was a military zone which no one could leave or enter without special permission. Now the Bedouins are free to come and go as they please, there is an air-conditioned bus to take them to Cairo. It was for them that I insisted on the tunnel under the Suez Canal. To make assimilation easier."

In among the young plants stands a house where the wind, which blows eagerly and virtually incessantly through this valley, meets with little resistance. The walls and the roof are woven, so that the interior is cool and shielded from the sun. Dozens of Persian carpets cover the floor. The low tables have been laid with care, and to judge by the large number of cushions, nearly a hundred guests are expected. Sadat has invited the sheikhs to a banquet. Suddenly, without anyone in the camp really having noticed, they are here – in their white gallabiahs, their ekals, the headscarves held in place with one or two black or colourful rings, and their faces etched deep by sun and wind. No one speaks. Closer inspection reveals that a number of soliders have mixed with the Bedouins, along with one woman, her head and arms covered, as tradition demands. Mrs. Sadat's progressive ideas have not yet penetrated here. At the Rais' table is the commander-in-chief of the Third Egyptian Army, General Osman, governor of the Sinai, once the commander of the Suez offensive, and the oldest sheikh, the moral leader of all the tribal chiefs. He is more than a hundred years old and fought in the First World War. He is small, frail and desiccated, but behind his Western spectacles his eyes are still lively. A remarkable guest among all these Muslims is the bishop of the monastery of Saint Catherine. A Greek, like all the other monks in this remote place of pilgrimage, he came here on foot and has nothing to ask the President. In his brown habit and long beard, he seems far removed from earthly concerns, and does not participate in the political discussions during the meal. Just as the others do, he tears pieces of meat from the lamb lying in the middle of the white rug, and he eats rice balls with his hands, in the Arab way. There are pickled peppers and carrots, dishes full of sweet cakes, Oriental *petit-fours*. The tea the servants bring round is also sweet. Sadat hardly tastes the food. He smokes his pipe intently while his guests gnaw their meat, drinks tea with honey instead of sugar and quaffs a salty drink in one gulp. The crickets make the most noise during this banquet, which lasts barely three-quarters of an hour.

In the dark, in front of the house, Sadat goes down on his knees again, and once more this man's amazing discipline becomes clear. Walking, massage, relaxation, Koran-reading, prayer, more Koran-reading. There is a time for everything in his day which no event, no circumstance of geography, can change.

Sadat has learned from history that discipline and regularity are essential in order to gain and keep power. Every politician organizes his life, but few stand in such close communion with the immaterial as Sadat.

"My father never eats lamb, he finds it too greasy and heavy. Roasted meat and chicken are better for his figure," says Sadat's youngest daughter Jehan, who is accompanying him on this trip. The President seldom travels without one or more members of his family, who usually seem to have little to do. Jehan did not eat with the distinguished guests as she had not brought a long-sleeved blouse with her. Anyway, she prefers playing backgammon with one of the guards. She behaves in a very Western manner, yet she was married at fifteen like most Egyptian girls. Besides security officers and secretaries, Sadat's entourage always includes doctors. Among them a surgeon and a cardiologist, who declares that Sadat's heart is in perfect condition and that the President exaggerates when he talks about his heart attacks in 1960 and 1970. Simply caused by temporary tension, he says. This would seem to make the cardiologist superfluous, but the man presumably wants to keep alive a myth surrounding the President.

In this region the sun rises at half-past four. Black donkeys bray and search for food among the soldiers wrapped in blankets, who have slept on the ground in the open air. It is still cool, but no one seems to want to take advantage of this lull between biting cold and murderous heat to engage in any activities. In the hills the commandos who keep watch over the Presidential camp extinguish the last fires. They are called 'Rangers', who live on snakes and lizards and do not know what to make of us when we climb up the rocks to get a better view.

"There, across the valley, I will build a synagogue, a Christian church and a mosque, next to one another. Proof of Egypt's desire to make all men brothers." Sadat said this yesterday, pointing to an open spot at the base of a steep mountain. He also wants to be buried there in all simplicity. Stones have been placed in the sand to form an Arabic text.

The monastery of Saint Catherine is waking up. In the luxurious gardens Bedouins of the Jebeliya tribe are already at work; they have worked so many years for the Greek Orthodox monks that they regard themselves as half Greek. They have also adopted some Christian habits, but are fasting while the monks are having their breakfast. Cypresses line the path leading to the wall behind which the monks' cells lie in this Biblical peace. Off to one side stands a whitewashed house that might have been a church; inside it are the bones of deceased monks, their skulls in a tidy pile behind a chickenwire gate. The stench is terrible.

The Rais never tires of talking about the Sinai. He does not seem to give the slightest consideration to the problems of the Bedouins, its present inhabitants. Do they play a role in his plans for a 'green revolution'? Sadat seems unconcerned about their opinion, but certainly his irrigation projects and dreams of urbanization will corrode social structures in the Sinai and disrupt the Bedouins' normal way of life. The consequence could be spiritual genocide, albeit in the distant future. "We have tremendous plans for this area," he says, indicating the virgin plains, "the exploitation of oil for a start. The gas produced will supply a power station, and the amount of coal under the ground here is so large that we will never have to worry about energy. We want to bring Egyptians from the Nile delta to cultivate suitable spots in the desert. The village named after my birthplace, Mit Abu el Kom Sinai, will be the home of 3,000 experts working on experiments in irrigation and agriculture. By the way, so much has happened since the Israelis left that when their minister Sharon visited us, he said he could not believe his eyes."

As if to lend credence to his enthusiasm, we take off in a column of Presidential jeeps, some flown over especially for the occasion, and drive to a nearby settlement. There architects show us where new buildings are going to be built. Drawings are unfolded while the women of the village, draped in black, stare curiously at these unexpected visitors. It is too hot to stay long, and Sadat retreats to his helicopter, which brings him to the small airstrip where he continues his journey to Suez, the afflicted city.

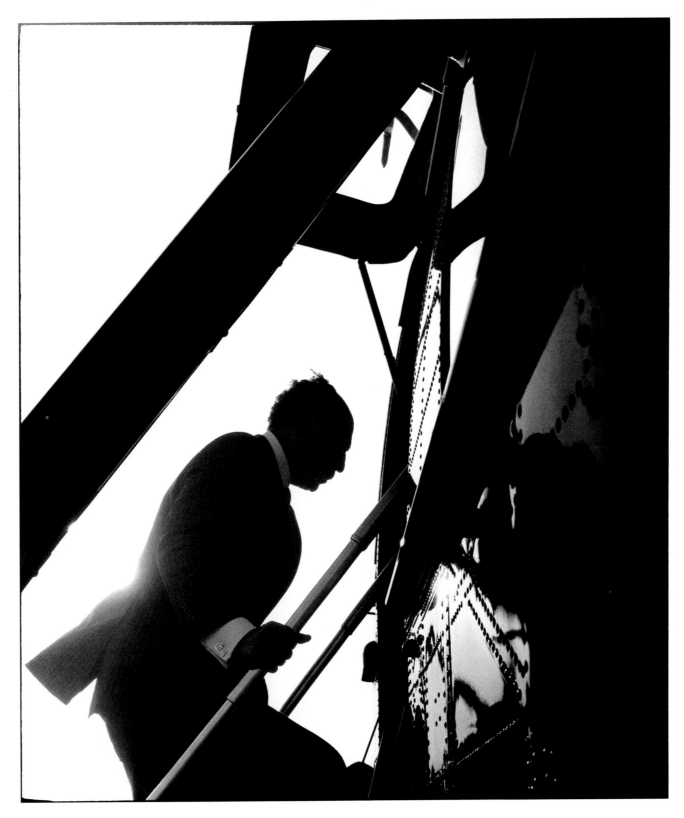

Taking off

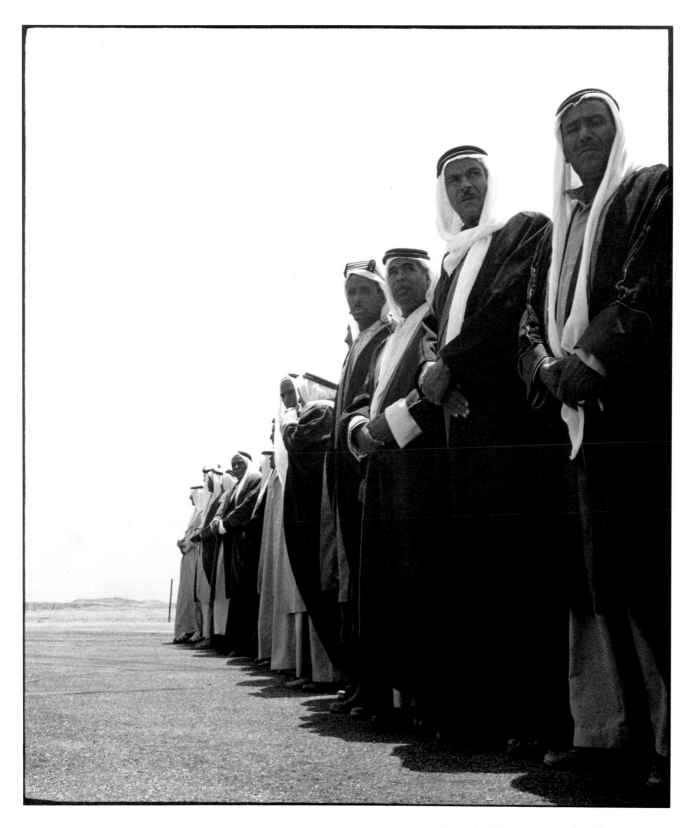

Guard of honour at a landing en route

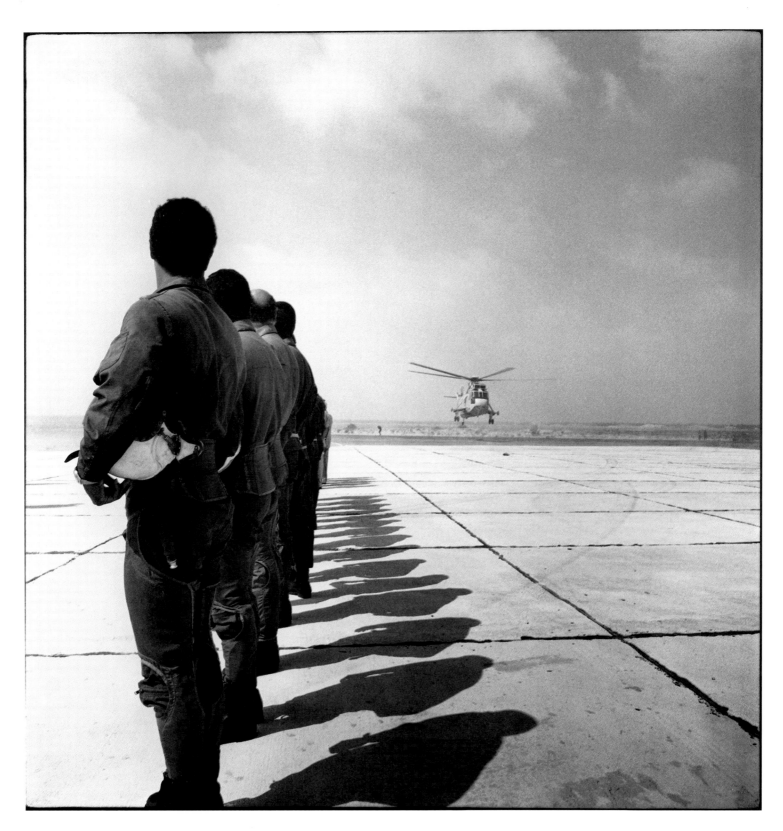

Bedouin sheikhs at his arrival in Sinai

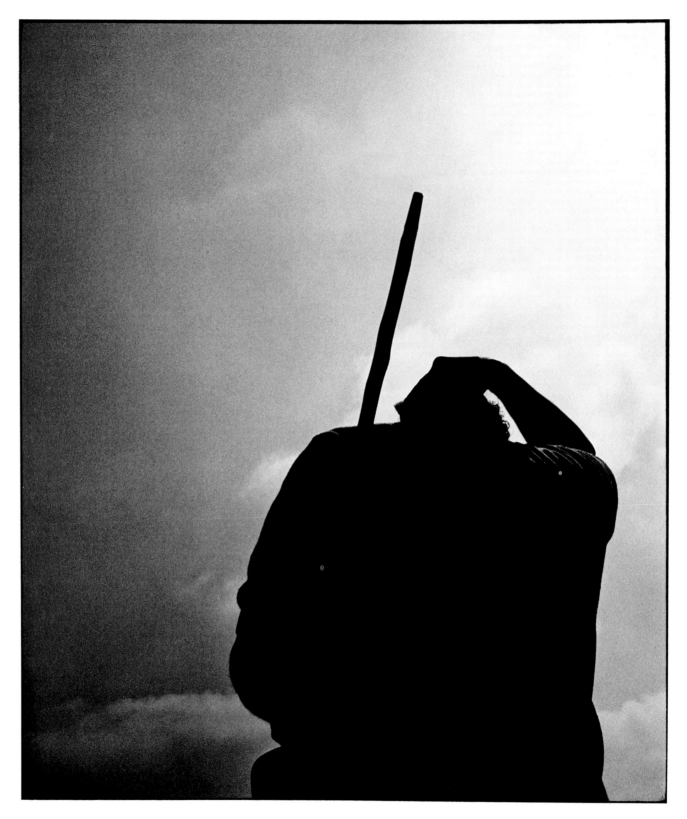

Midday heat

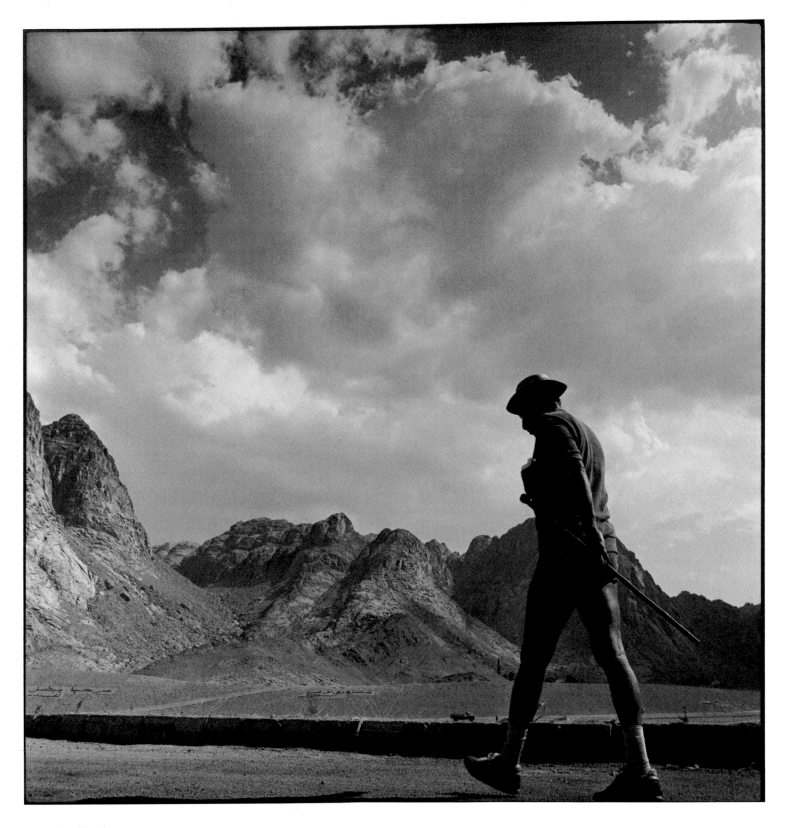

In "his" Sinai

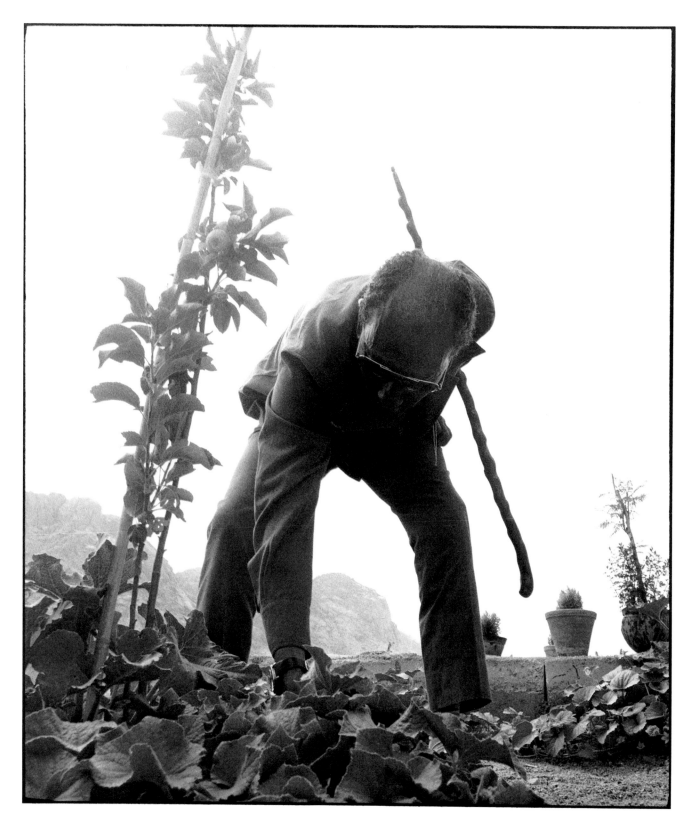

His own harvest

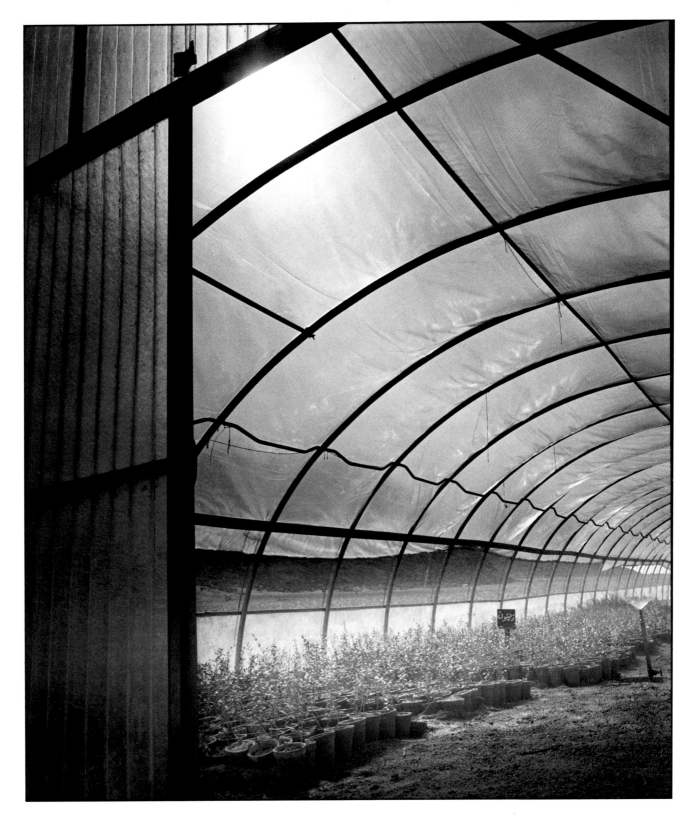

The greenhouse

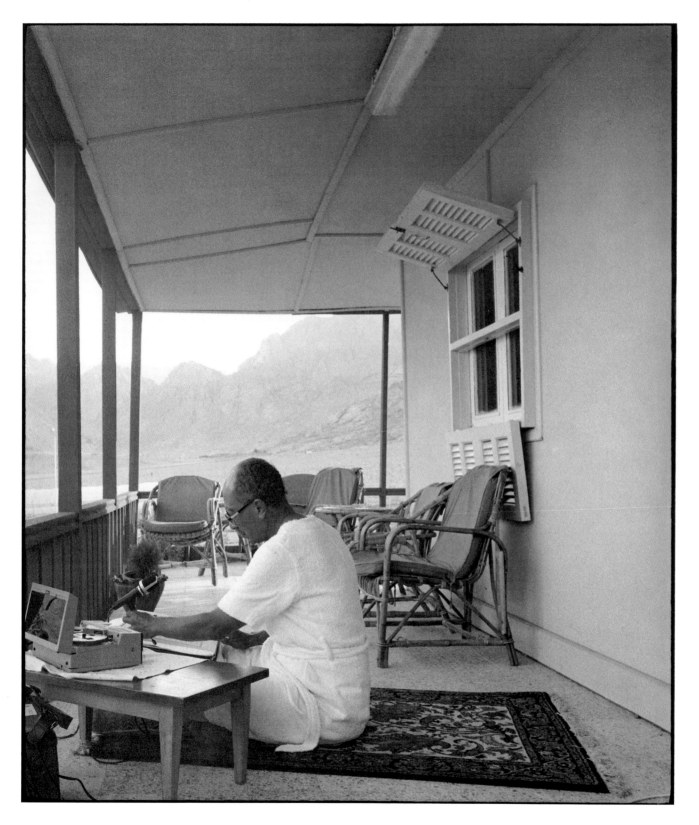

Modernism and tradition

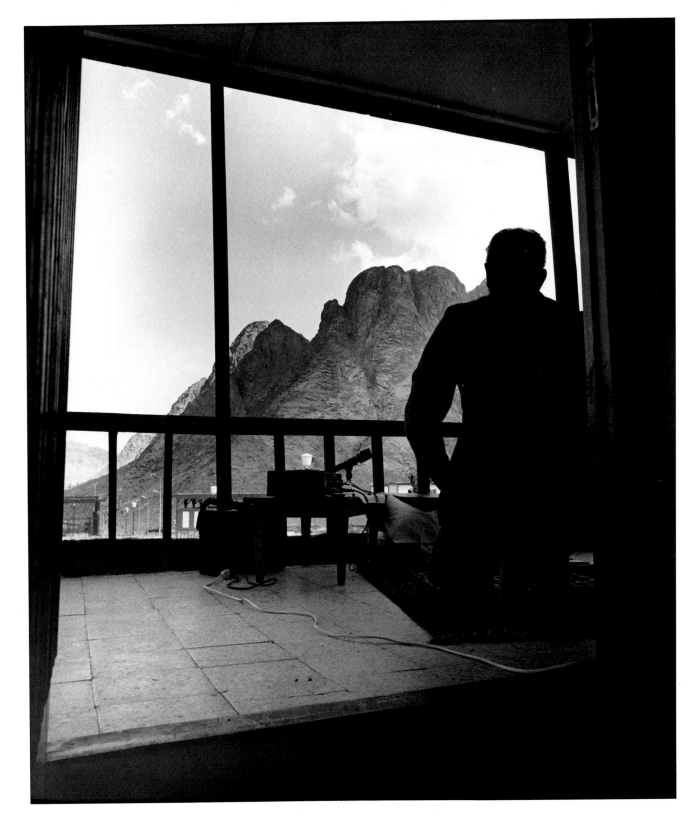

Prayer on Mt Sinai

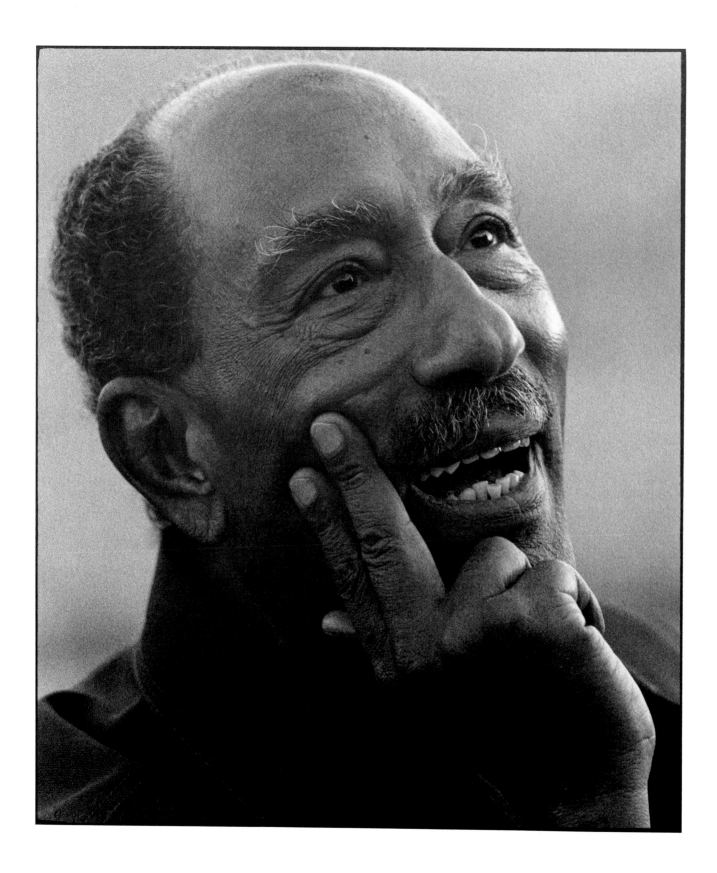

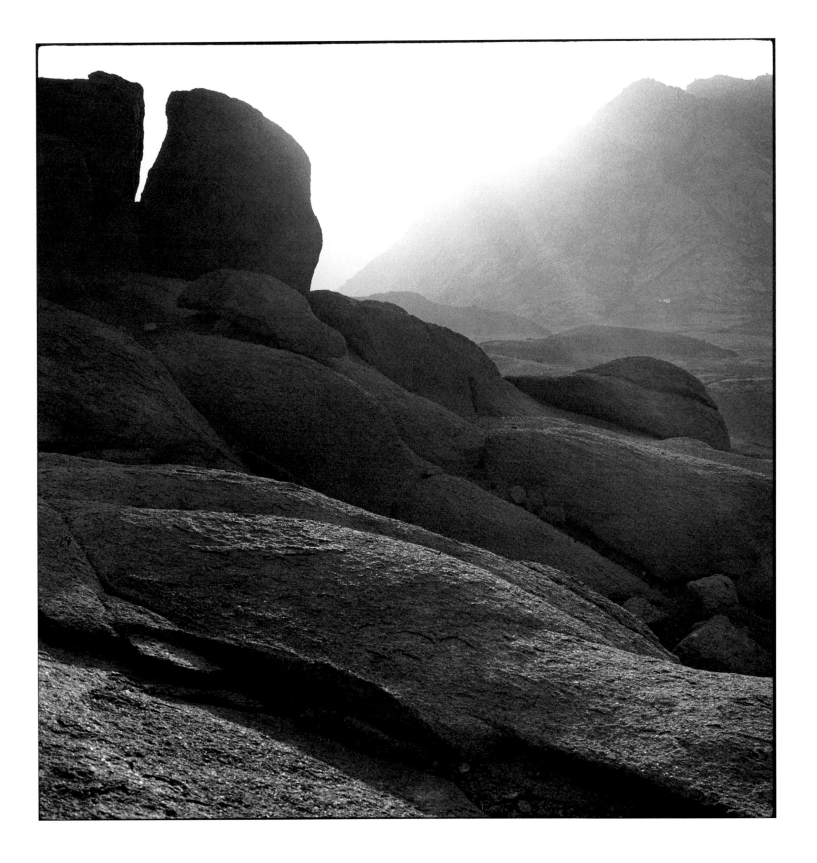

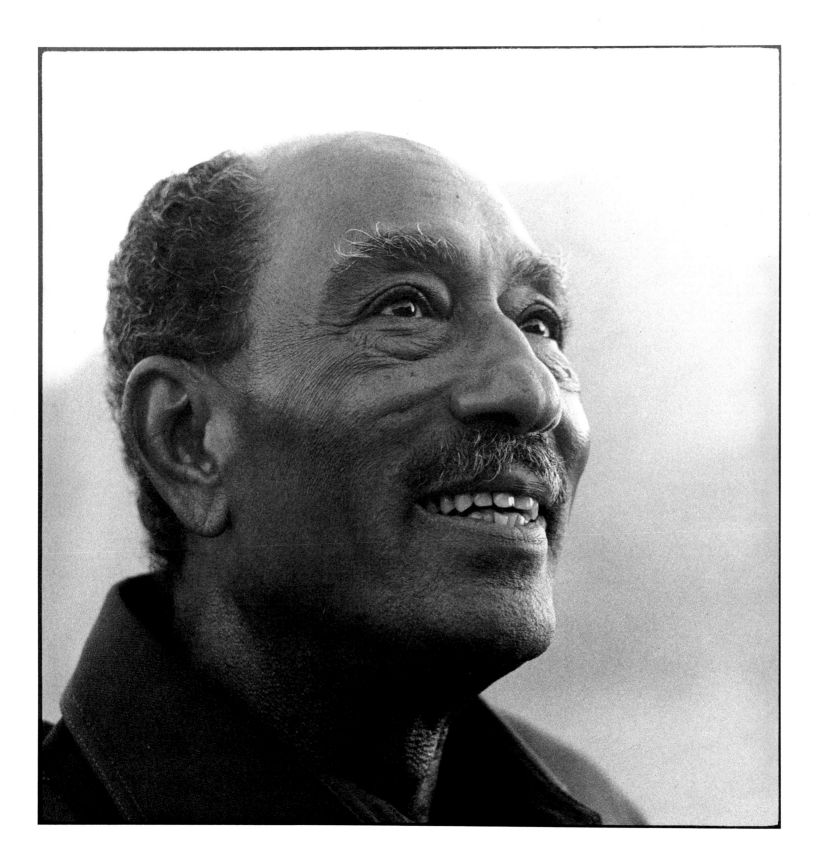

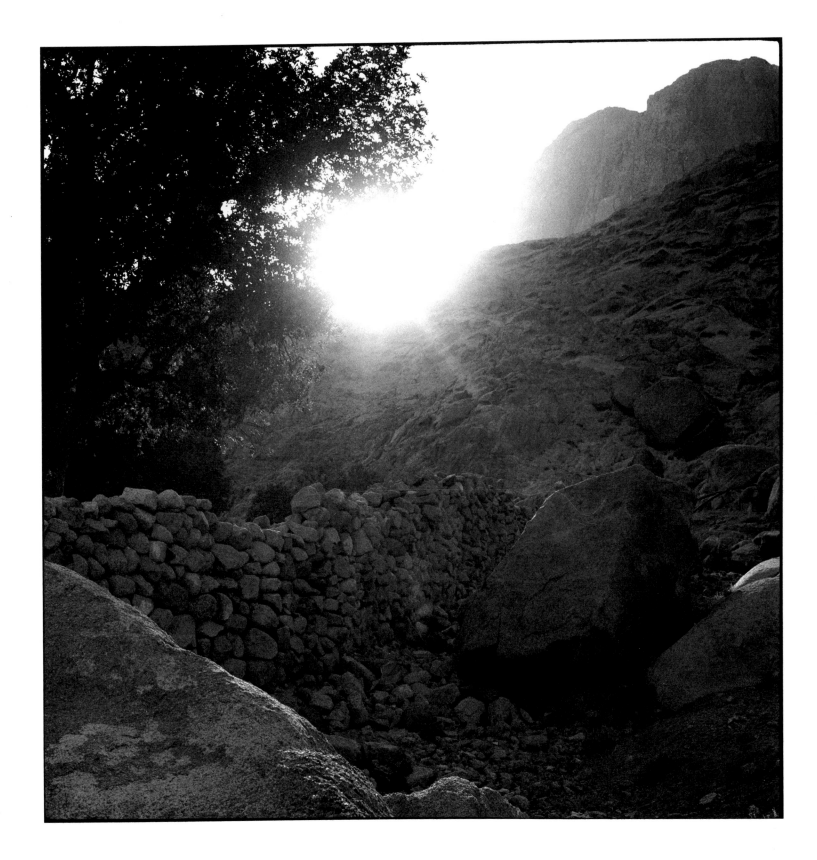

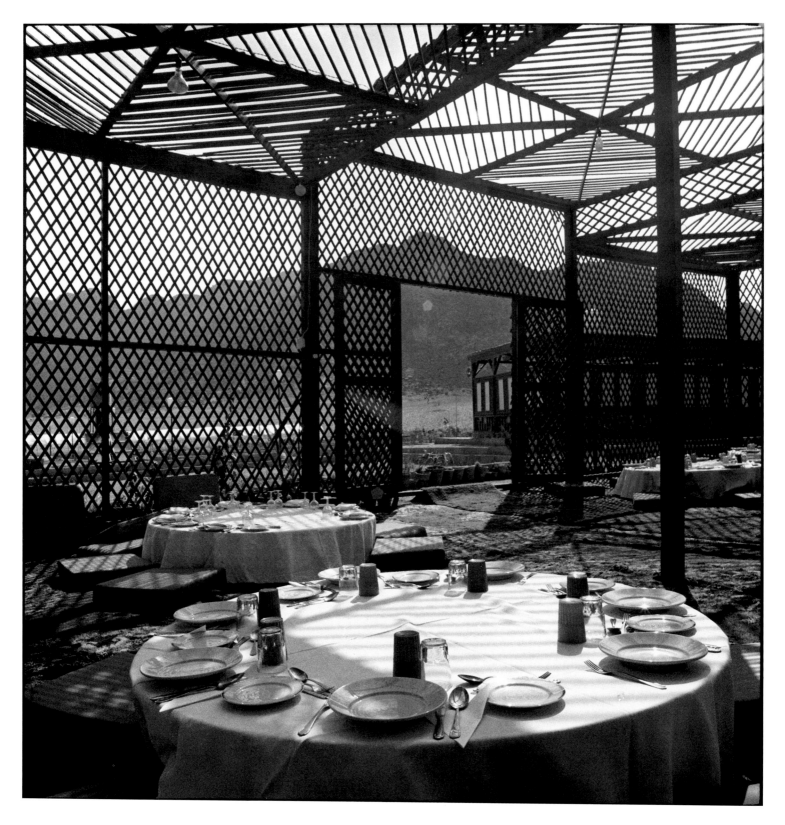

Before the banquet

III Travels

It was a problem for the media: should they call the meeting-place of President Sadat and Prime Minister Begin Ofira, as the Israelis have renamed it, or, looking into the future, Sharm-el-Sheikh, as it used to be called? The two politicians meet for the first time in a year and a half, this time at the insistence of Begin, who wants to show shortly before the elections in his country that he too is an architect of peace. What motivated Sadat to come? After all, it is no secret that he could conceive of other, more liberal leaders for Israel, and that it may not be exactly in his own interest to help Begin this way.

Contemplatively Sadat looks out of the window at the Sinai while we fly low above it. Like Begin on the other side, he is preparing his role: laughter, pats on the back, hail-fellow-well-met, to show the world that the two countries get along famously. This time, too, they manage pretty well. The Egyptian Boeing parks alongside the Israeli plane, and as we get out Begin is already standing on the concrete to receive his guest – for Sadat is still a guest here. Since we are not wearing badges, an Israeli security man grabs us by the collar and asks, "Do you want to get killed?" An Israeli soldier, nervously carrying out his orders, pushes the barrel of his machine gun at us, and it is only thanks to the intervention of an Egyptian security officer that we are allowed to walk on with the delegation.

The two statesmen take a helicopter to a villa on the sea, where they discuss the explosive situation in Lebanon. The Syrian invasion is sharply condemned. Sadat asks Israel to have patience and to allow the American negotiator Philip C. Habib more time to find a solution to the crisis and to establish a cease-fire. In the meantime a protest is being staged outside, in the water, against the return of the Sinai to Egypt. The demonstrators are from Yamit, Jewish immigrants who do not want to be sent back to Israel from their village, as Sadat has announced he will do after April 1982. He is afraid conflicts will arise if the Jewish settlements are not evacuated....The demonstrators draw the attention of the international press until they are summarily carted off by Israeli soldiers.

When the talks are finished we fly back to Sadat's residence in Ismaelia. We do not see him again, as he wishes to remain among his intimates. We are given accommodation in the guesthouse of the 'Authorities of the Suez Canal', the former house of Ferdinand de Lesseps, architect of the Canal.

The trip to London on the way to the United States gets off to a bad start for the security officers. After Sadat, his wife, children, grandchildren and accompanying ministers leave the Presidential plane, two huge bobbies move into place at the bottom of the stairway and let no one pass, no matter how the bodyguards and doctors push and swear. (Now a certain element of rancor against the British comes to the surface.) The stolid policemen stand their ground, and after repeated questioning all they will say is that their Egyptian colleagues may not leave the plane as long as they are armed. In fact, they themselves are not armed.

Furious, the Egyptians surrender their most important means of self-defence and get to work, feeling half exposed. During the entire visit they keep looking around fearfully, and it seems unlikely that they would know what to do in an emergency.

A car with a chauffeur and telephone, and a room in that most elegant of elegant hotels, Claridge's, prove that we have now been accepted as members of the Egyptian delegation. No shoving behind fences, no punching and swearing. A blue-black badge is supposed to open all doors, but when we arrive the next morning in the 'Quadrangle', the courtyard of the Ministry of Foreign Affairs, to witness Sadat's official reception by Margaret Thatcher, things do not turn out as planned.

A gentleman from the protocol department mistakenly interprets our dark suits as a sign of rank and places us next to the British Prime Minister. The make-up and the half-length beige calfskin gloves are so typically English that the Iron Lady looks like a caricature of herself. But her unconstrained behaviour makes up for it. She jokes with the officer of the Royal Guards, shuffles her feet and complains about her busy schedule. "Receptions and more recep-

tions," she whispers, smiling, and looks at her watch: Sadat is late, fourteen minutes late to be precise. Arrogance? Anger at being met at the airport by 'only' two unknown civil servants? No, more likely absent-mindedness. He seems rather distracted when he finally gets out of a Rolls-Royce, and as he greets Mrs. Thatcher, he discovers that he is still holding his pipe. Shouts, waves, a bodyguard comes running up to relieve him of the smoking gear; eyebrows are raised for an instant, but then matters proceed according to protocol. Sadat in a pinstripe suit, without his cane, which would have been not at all inappropriate here, inspects the guard. In spite of the heat, which seems to follow us everywhere, none of the busby-wearers faints. The soldiers' sweat drops unheeded onto the black toes of their shoes, which look like upturned noses. The guardsmen on parade turn and salute geometrically and synchronously under the windows of Lord Carrington's offices.

Mrs. Thatcher leads her guest through a passageway to 10 Downing Street, where she stands on the doorstep, takes Sadat by the arm and forces him to look into the camera.

"From the moment that the British Minister of Foreign Affairs Lord Carrington visited Egypt, I knew the British were intent on working towards a solution of the Palestinian problem in the Middle East. Now that they are at the head of the Council of Ministers of the Common Market, they can also exert more influence on their partners and infuse the European initiative with new life. I said this a few months ago in Strasbourg: the Camp David agreements together with the European initiative can solve the Palestinian issue. London must try to convince the Americans to include the Palestinians in the negotiations as well."

As always, Sadat exudes self-confidence. All day long he receives politicians, representatives of the Egyptian community and journalists in the Ambassador's residence, where he and his family are staying. The Palestinians demonstrating in front of the Embassy on South Audley Street, who alternately accuse Sadat of deceit and ask for his help, try to push their spokesmen through a police cordon, and when that fails, the message is delivered with the help of a megaphone.

During lunch at Buckingham Palace, Sadat talks at length with Queen Elizabeth II, but no one is able to hear, as none of the members of the delegation participate. The Queen does not receive her guest at the door, but inside the room, and Sadat must wait for her and not the other way round. This is quite a surprise for the accompanying bodyguards, who are not at all taken with this country.

Washington, August 4 – 10, 1981.

The American government has had little time so far to concern itself with foreign affairs. The domestic economy has overshadowed everything else. If and when the Middle East has been mentioned, it is only incidentally and as applied to Russian ambitions in the Persian Gulf: the Palestinian problem seemed of secondary importance. Most of the Arab leaders, however, including Sadat, take quite the opposite view of priorities, although they also worry about the open support the Soviet Union is giving certain countries. Unless a solution is found for the Palestinian issue, unless the Palestinians are given self-determination in some form or other, at least in the Gaza strip and on the west bank of the Jordan, an accord is hardly feasible. The divided, conservative Arab world cannot shake its fist at the Soviet Union until this matter is settled. In the course of our talks Sadat keeps repeating that his task will only be completed when he has fulfilled this part of the promise made in the Camp David agreements. "That can only happen if the Israelis and the Americans are prepared to negotiate with the Palestinians. I will put this to President Reagan," says the Rais before departing for the United States. But Reagan somewhat disappoints Sadat by adhering to his view that the PLO is a terrorist organisation and can therefore never be a partner in negotiations. Sadat seems to have expected this attitude. In spite of it there is no lack of mutual praise, particularly of the role Sadat and the United States have played in the past.

Since Reagan became President, White House observers have noticed two things: first, that he is constantly acting, but mainly for the cameras and not for the microphones. Secondly, Presidential ceremony occupies a more important place than it did under most of his recent predecessors. The protocol department is kept busy before and during official occasions arranging the tiniest details of the cavalcade, the reception, the dinners, the table seating, the number of steps guests and host must take at a given moment. The country's grandeur must be reflected very clearly in the dignity of the ceremonies.

When Sadat and his wife leave Blair House, the luxurious accommodation for state visitors across from the White House, a security agent on the roof signals a colleague on the other side of the street. At that very moment President Reagan receives a signal to descend the stairs. The car transporting the Egyptian guests drives at exactly the right speed to arrive at the flight of marble steps behind the White House as the host is coming down to meet them. Perfect choreography, this ballet that works like a well-oiled machine under the direction of the Presidential staff. "The gentlemen wearing hats," says the lavishly executed program distributed to the guests, "are to lay them over their left shoulder in such a way that their hand covers their heart." While the national anthem is played, the Reagans, Vice-President George Bush and his wife, the Secretary of State and Mrs. Haig all place their right hands over their hearts, as do the other American guests. Twenty-one salutes are fired and martial music resounds over the lawn, steaming in the damp Washington heat. The guard of honor is inspected from the red and gold podium of honor, for security reasons.

Mrs. Sadat stands calmly on the lawn looking ironically at the nameplate on the ground which indicates exactly where she is meant to stand.

Behind the gold ropes separating the guests from the Heads of State unrest is breaking out in the inhuman heat. Men search for shadow under their wives' hats, make-up disintegrates from the ladies' faces.

Sadat's youngest daughter, Jehan, collapses and has to be taken off to a hospital. But the festivities go on. Fife-playing soldiers dressed in Revolutionary uniforms parade past the guests. Reagan laughs and looks remarkably fit, even next to Sadat, who continually wipes the perspiration from his forehead with a handkerchief. Reagan calls the Egyptian President an example for the entire world, "living proof that peace can be achieved", a "friend" and a "partner". It is noticeable that he speaks with his back to his guest, perhaps for the sake of the photographers. But Sadat steals the show with the words, "We shall both overcome . . ."

Drummers appear on the steps, trumpets blare, banners wave, and then the company retires. In the Oval Office we are allowed to see Sadat and Reagan for a moment more, ill-at-ease in their joviality.

The official dinner given for Sadat in the White House is extremely formal. In the hall, an orchestra plays "Hail America" and "Golden Friendship" while the two couples, preceded by representatives of the various branches of the armed forces in dress uniform, descend the majestic staircase. The Reagans gives almost the impression of monarchs, Anwar Sadat and his wife appear as modest, laughing guests in the background.

Blair House is an island of tranquillity, where portraits of American presidents and authors keep watch in the salons and library. Visitors are accompanied by dozens of security men, who can be recognized by their too-tight suits, the tiny microphone up their sleeves and the earphone which is connected almost invisibly to a transmitter in their breast pocket. They bitch incessantly at their Egyptian colleagues, who are either standing in the wrong place or absent altogether because they are off sneaking a tidbit from the plates of sandwiches. Waiters are serving the high-ranking guests, who are waiting in the salons until the Egyptian President, with his overloaded schedule, has time for them. Ex-President Gerald Ford warmly greets the personnel and makes the rounds while waiting for his 'great friend' Sadat. It is all very jolly when the two finally fall into each other's arms: a friend is a friend forever – whether it is Ford, or Richard Nixon, who is also scheduled for a meeting, or Jimmy Carter, whom Sadat is to visit in Plains.

America's leading politicians, Alexander Haig, Minister of Defense Caspar Weinberger and Vice-President Bush, have to wait their turn to greet the Egyptian President. The meetings are informal tête-à-têtes that the public never gets to see, because the media have been refused entry into Blair House. Some do their homework (Haig), others lean back in their chairs and talk about jogging (Bush), others make jokes and act jovial (Ford). Weinberger speaks the longest with Sadat: about extra arms for Egypt, which wants to be regarded as an equally valuable and trustworthy partner in the Middle East as Israel, about Egypt, that 'island of peace' (as Sadat calls it) among the turbulent waves; about the fratricide in Lebanon, the oppression in Syria and Iraq, the violent explosions in Iran. He convinces Weinberger to give Egypt more arms, delivered sooner than expected. That is some satisfaction, even if Sadat cannot bring home immediate prospects for continuing the peace negotiations.

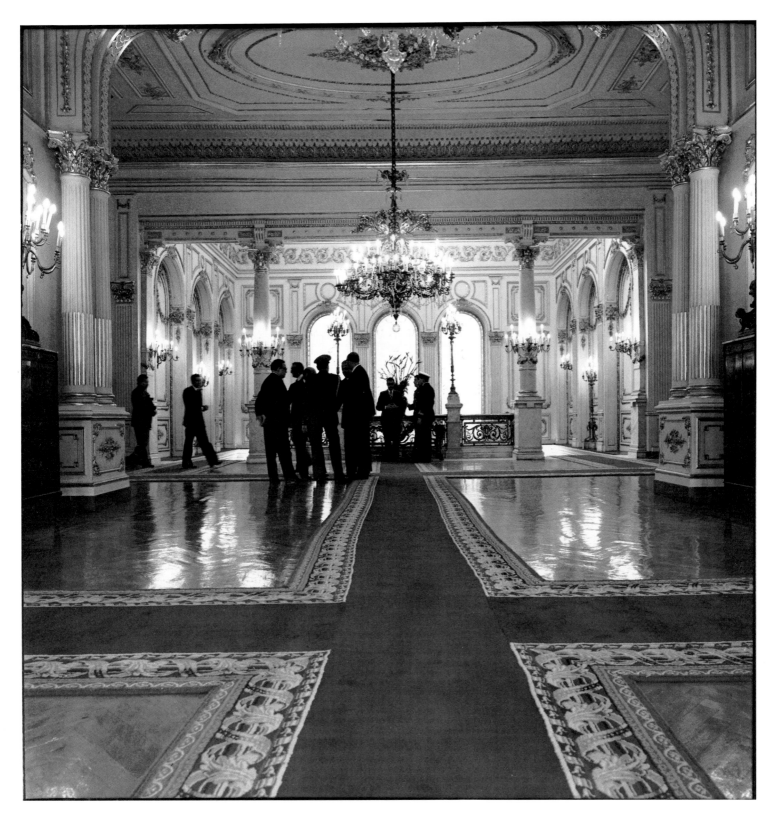

Abdin Palace, Cairo

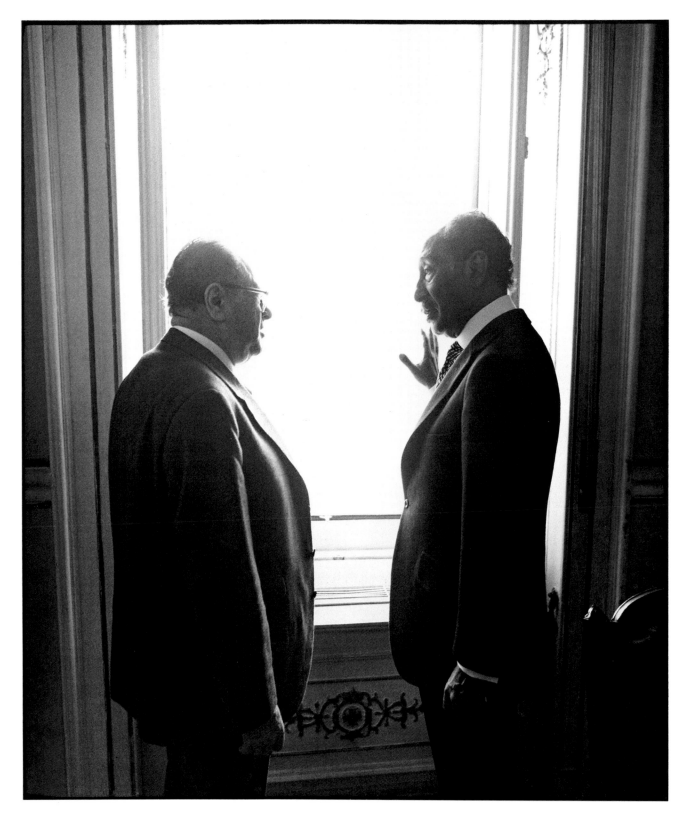

With Bruno Kreisky in Cairo

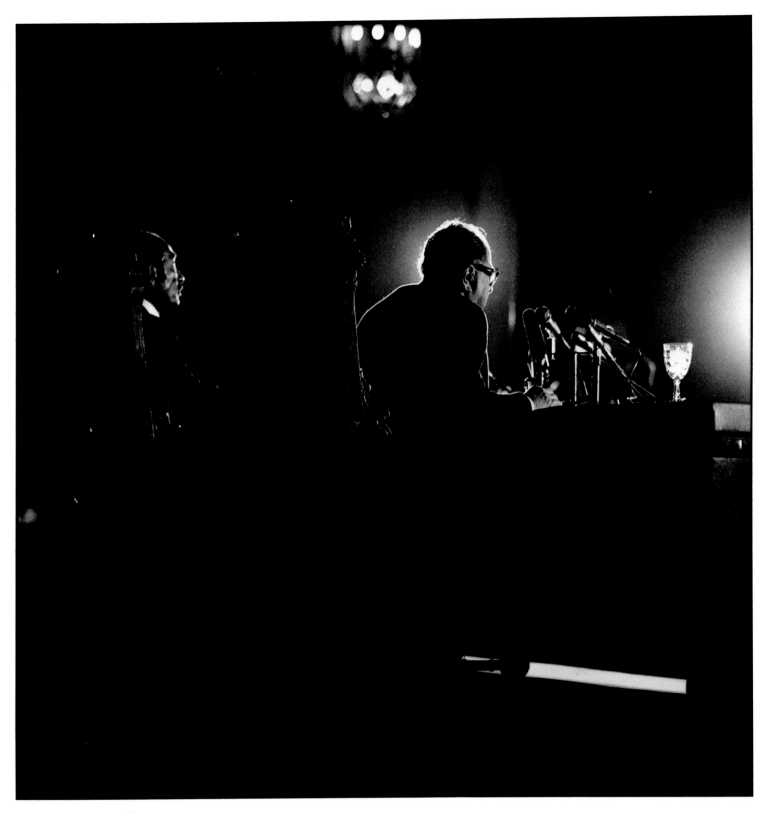

Press conference

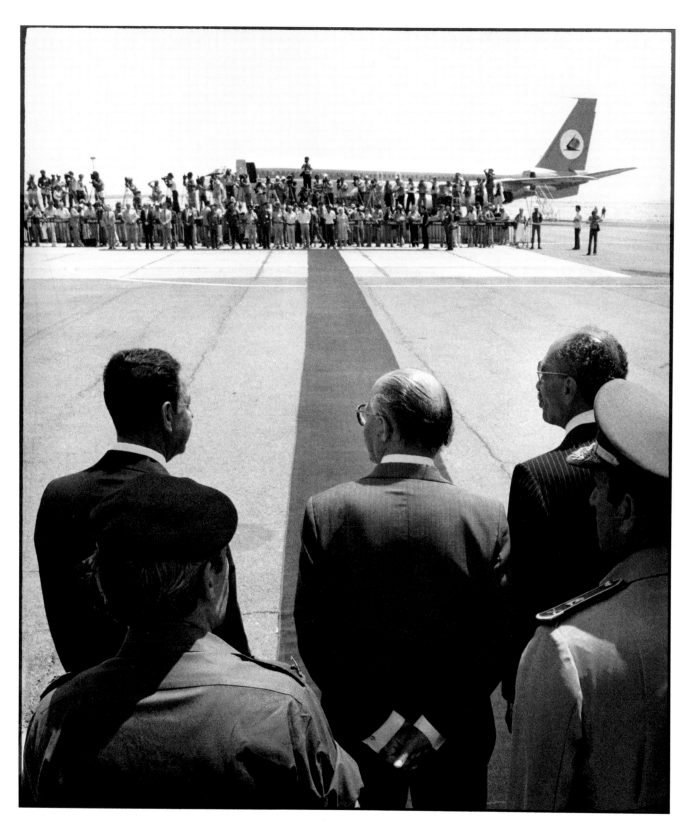

Guests of honour and members of the press

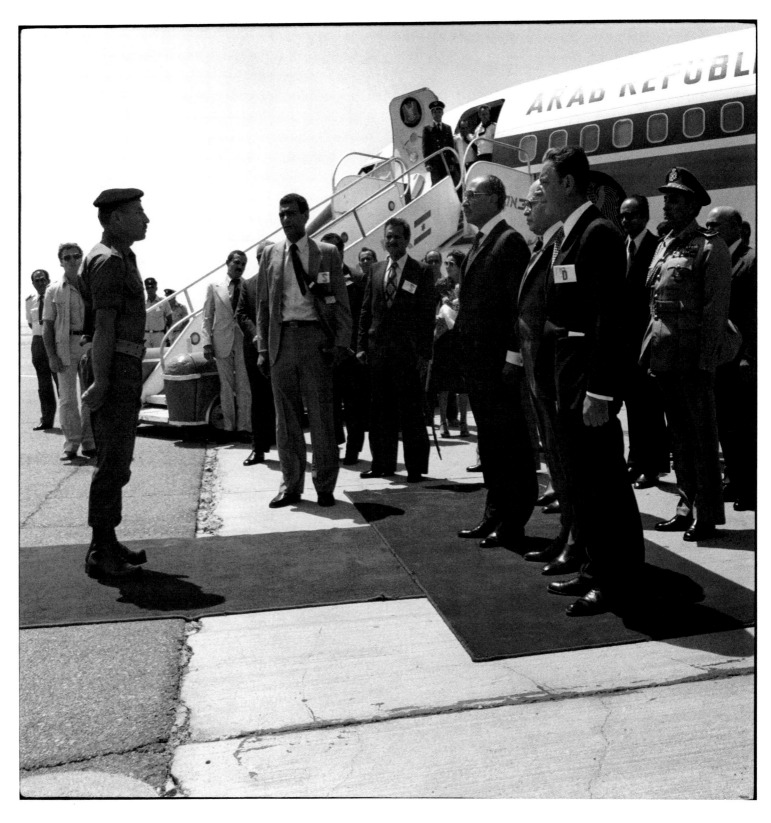

With Menachem Begin at Sharm el-Sheikh

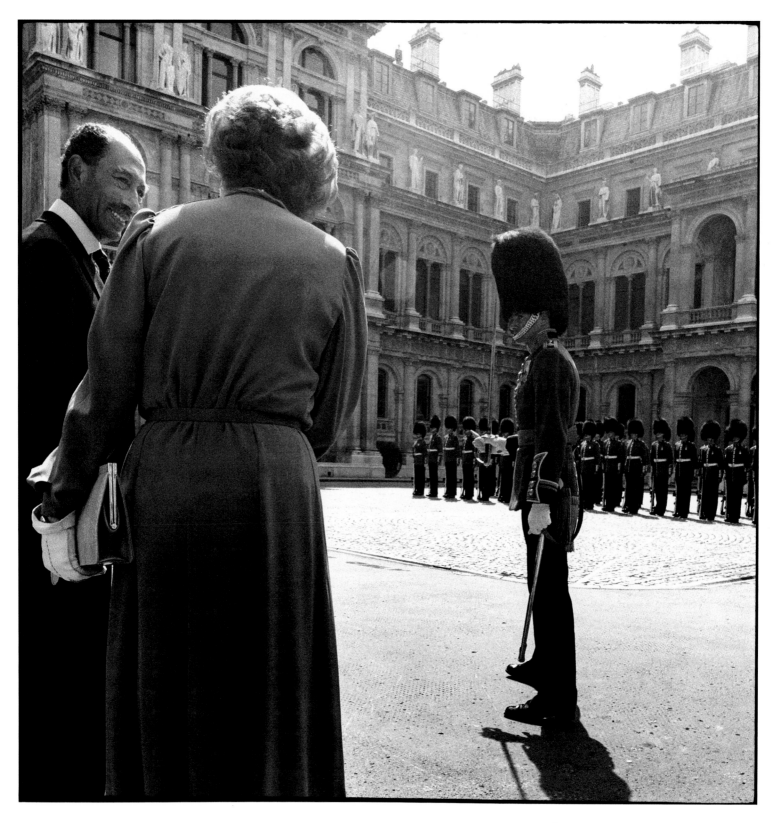

With Margaret Thatcher in London

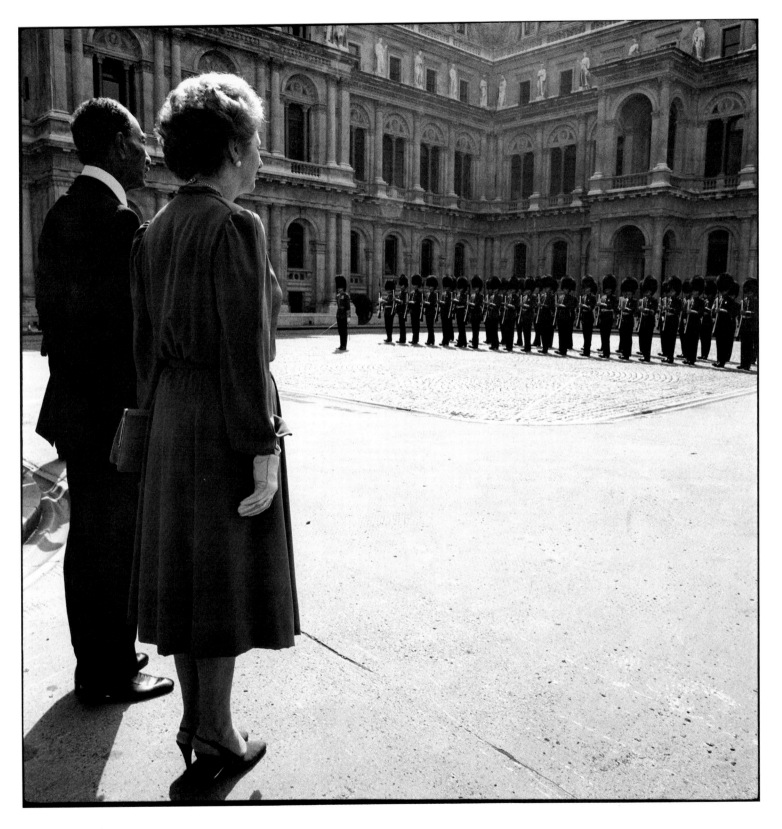

National anthem

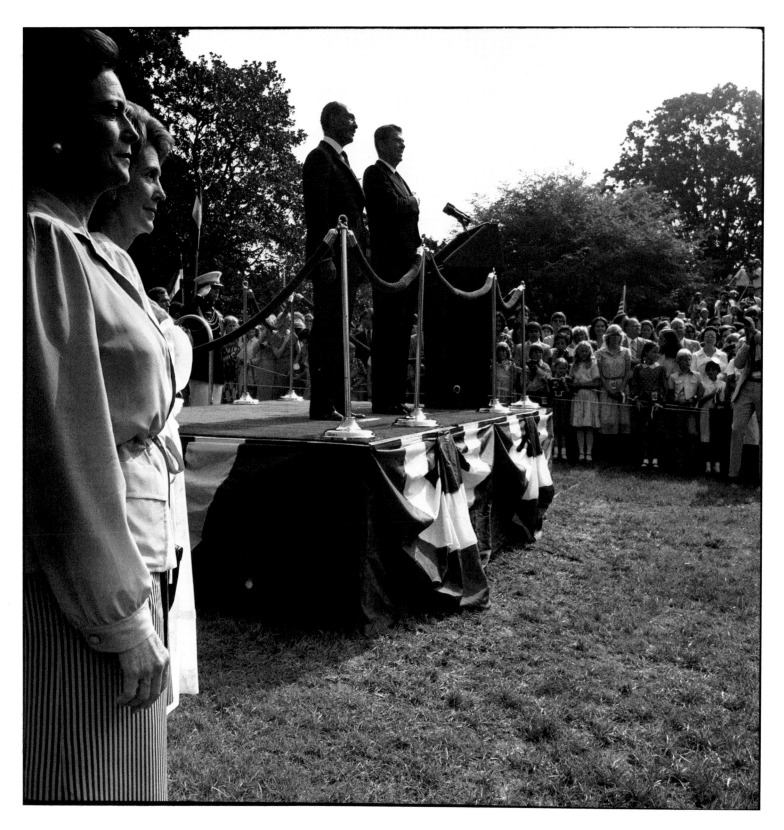

In the garden of the White House

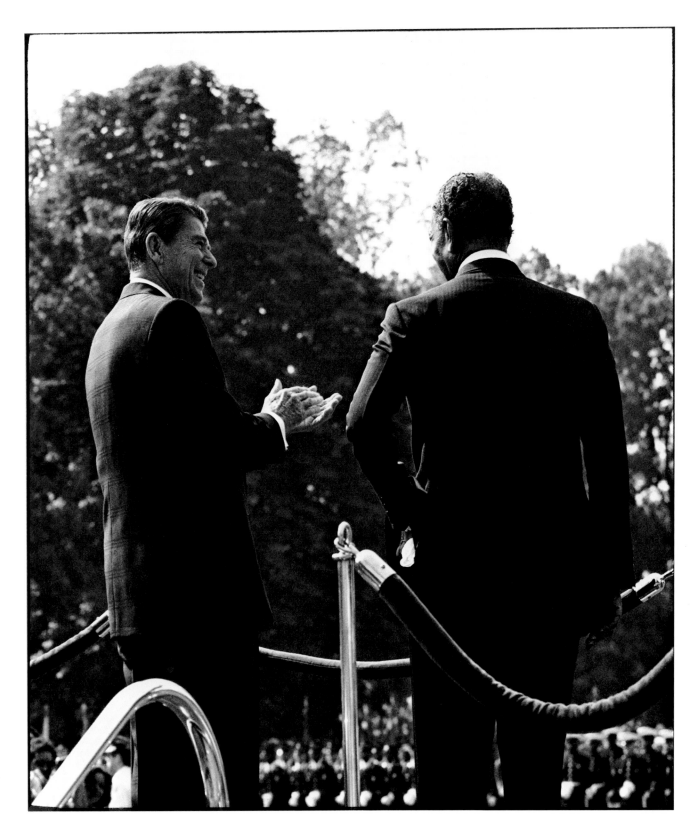

With Ronald Reagan

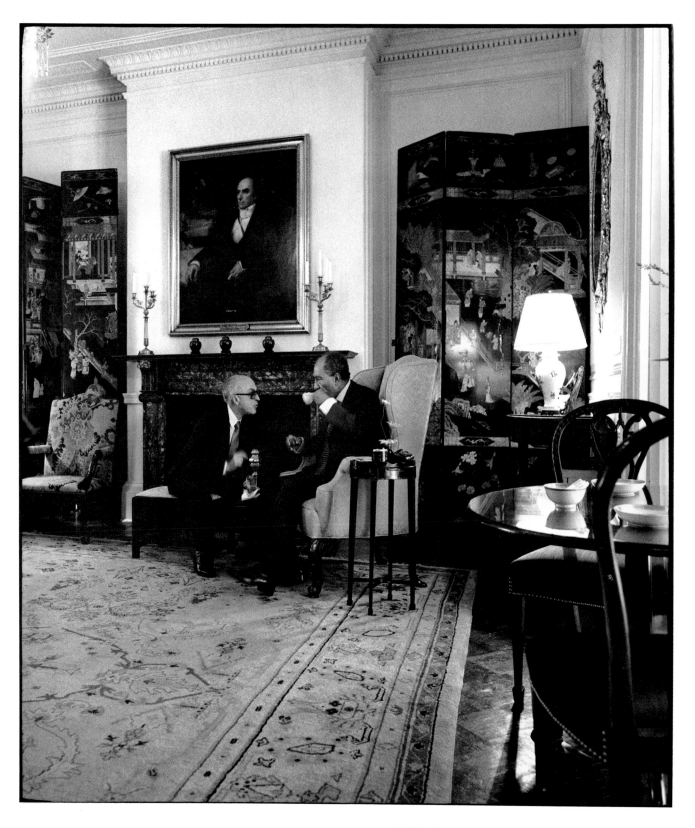

With the Egyptian ambassador at Blair House

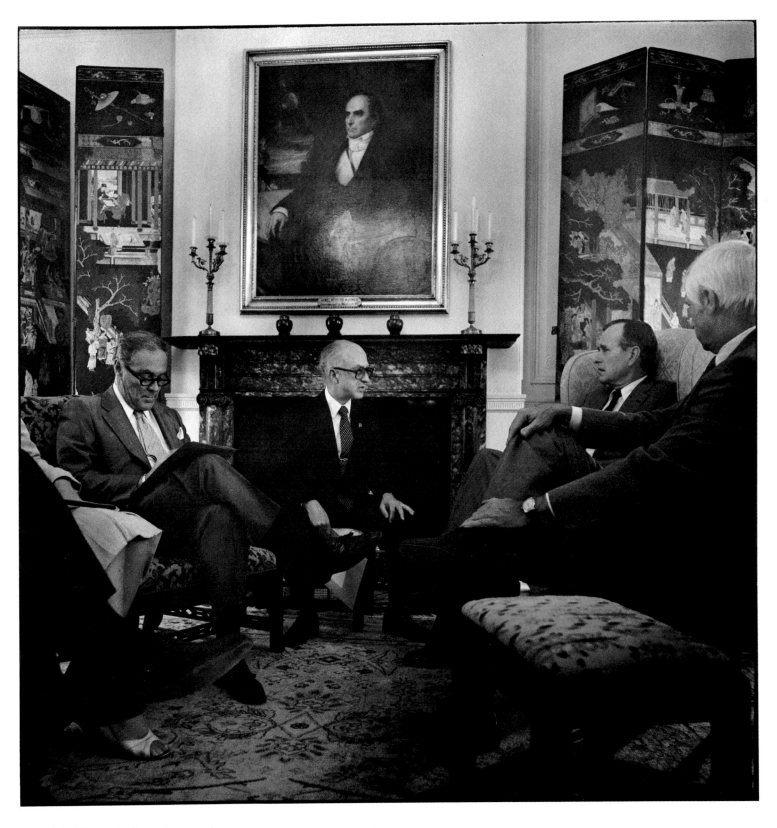

At Blair House before the meetings

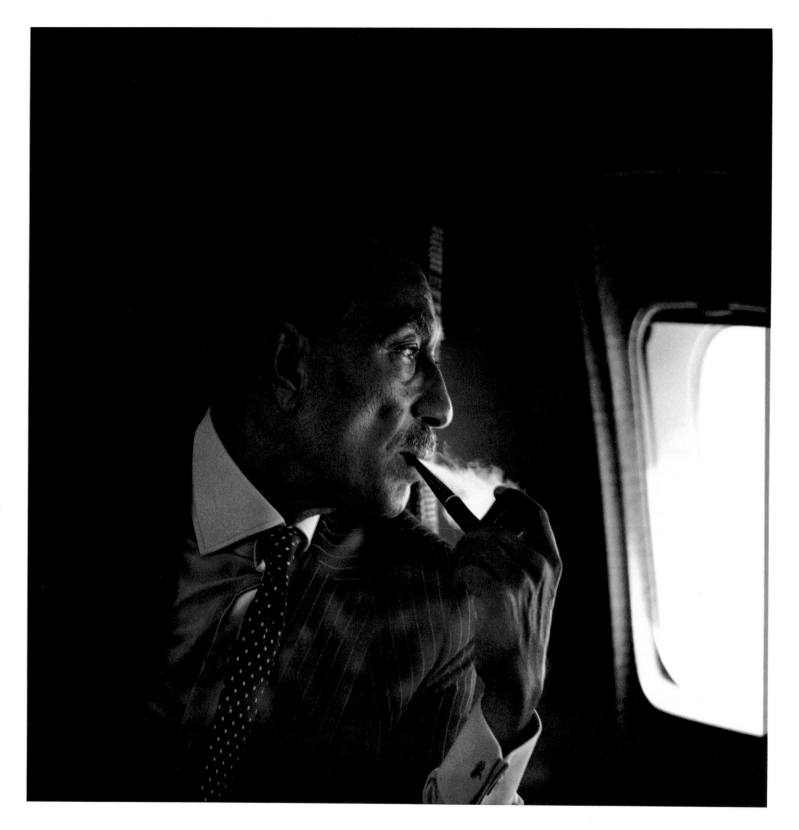

On the plane

Epilogue

In mid-August, on our flight back from the United States to Cairo, a stop-over at Salzburg had been planned. Chancellor Kreisky, however, warned Sadat that he could not guarantee his safety as a Syrian extremist organization was reported to be planning an attempt on his life. From the President's inner circle we learned about rumours of unrest in Egypt which caused him to return to Cairo directly. A few weeks later he had some 1500 people arrested – intellectuals, journalists, religious leaders, and other opponents, real and presumptive. A few newspapers were closed down. Apparently the opposition had voiced its criticism too loudly. From outside the country, the steps taken by Sadat seemed, to say the least, undemocratic. What prompted him to these actions is a question only Middle East experts will be able to answer.

To us, these developments in Egypt proved that there was in fact more than just one Sadat: not only the pipe-smoking harbinger of peace but also the leader who would suffer no opposition as long as he could not control it. Would still tougher measures have strengthened his position, or saved his life? Perhaps they would not have made any great difference: the irredeemable act, unforgivable in the eyes of his Arab foes, had happened long ago – Sadat's historic journey to Jerusalem, his peace initiative with Israel. To quote the words he chose for his epitaph, he died for his principles – and only history will tell whether his efforts were in vain or not.

Among those who died alongside Anwar Sadat on that fateful 6th of October were men whom we had come to know and respect, and who had made valuable contributions to this book. We are deeply indebted to them as well as to other members of the late President's entourage.

This book was conceived as a series of snapshots contributing to a factual biography. We are both deeply grieved that the terrible event should have turned this documentation into a last farewell.

MUNICH, 12 OCTOBER 1981

Mark Blaisse
Konrad R. Müller

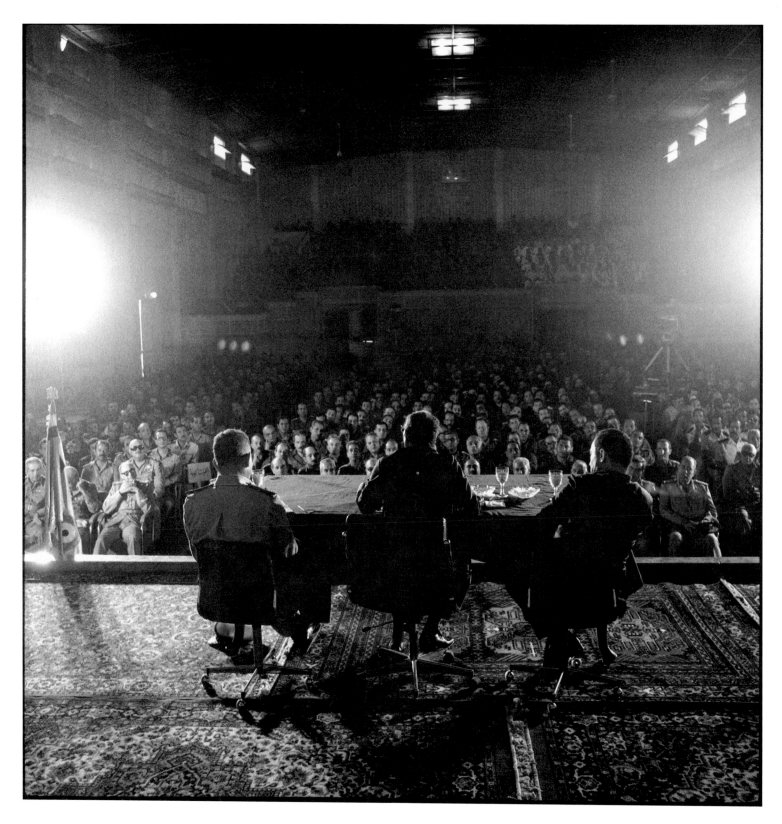

With the 2nd Army

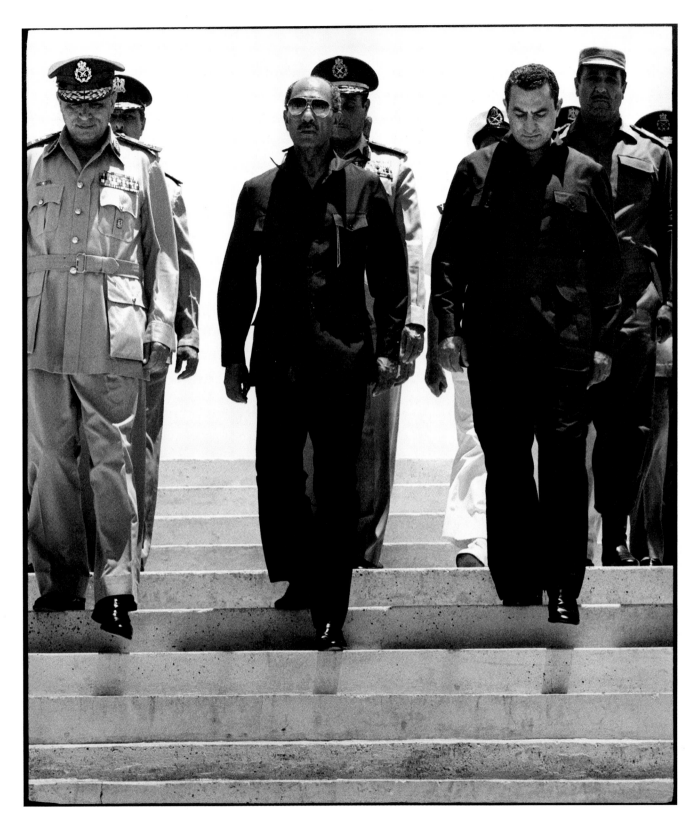

With his successor Hosni Mubarak

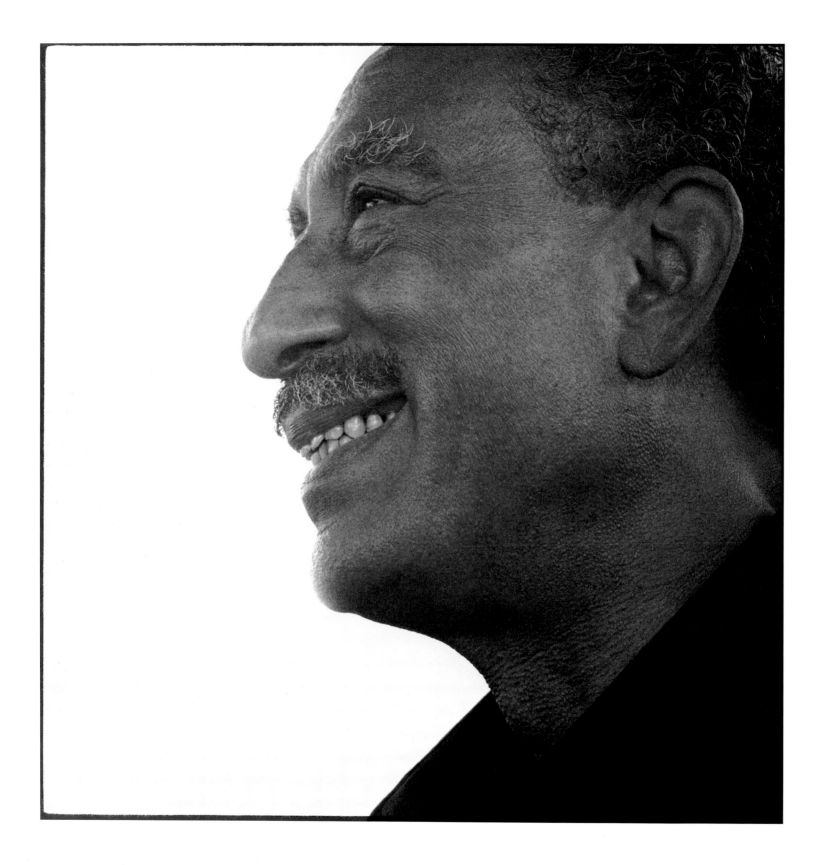

Biographical Note

Mahommed Anwar El-Sadat was born on 25 December 1918, the son of an Egyptian peasant and a Sudanese woman. At the Military Academy, he became friendly with Gamal Abdel Nasser, and as early as 1938 the two of them founded the Association of Free Officers which was to bring down King Farouk in 1952. In the Second World War Sadat, anti-British along with his friends, supported Germany and served some time in prison. In 1946 he was suspected of participating in the plot to murder the pro-British Finance Minister, Amin Osman; he was cleared only $2\frac{1}{2}$ years later.

Under President Nasser Sadat was Information Minister (1954-56), President of Parliament (1960-69), from 1962 General Secretary of the state party, the Arabic Socialist Union, and in 1969 Vice-President of the Union of Egypt and Syria.

Upon Nasser's death, Sadat succeeded him in October 1970. In May 1971 he brought to an end an internal political struggle for power by dismissing Vice-President Ali Sabri and other opponents in high state positions. By these means Sadat was able to ensure the support of the masses. At the end of 1971 he took over command of the Egyptian military forces.

After the fall of Ali Sabri, who was considered Moscow's man, Sadat broke off relations with the Soviet Union. In the summer of 1972 he ordered about 20,000 Soviet military advisers to leave the country, and in 1976 he announced cancellation of the friendship treaty with the Soviet Union. On 6 October 1973, the Israeli holy day of Yom Kippur, Egyptian and Syrian troops mounted a surprise offensive on Israel. Their aim was apparently to breach the boundaries established at the peace talks and to create a better position for later negotiations. The October War led to a military stalemate. By crossing the Suez Canal on a broad front, however, Sadat was able to give back to the Arab world a lost sense of self-confidence and to damage the myth of Israel's invincibility. In 1974 diplomatic relations with Washington, which had been broken off in 1967, were resumed. The disengagement of troops in the Sinai took place through the efforts of Secretary of State, Henry Kissinger.

Internally, Sadat brought about in the course of that year a certain liberalization. Press censorship was lifted, industry was opened to foreign capital and nationalization was rolled back. In 1975 the Suez Canal was reopened after an eight-year closure.

Sadat's internal political problems were not solved. In January 1977 there were demonstrations against planned price rises and the Army killed 60 people.

In November 1977 Sadat made his historic visit to Jerusalem; in September 1978 the Camp David agreements were ratified; and in March 1979 a peace treaty with Israel was signed, which called for the return of Sinai to Egypt. Shortly after Camp David, Sadat and the Israeli Prime Minister Begin shared the Nobel Peace Prize. But in the Arab world, Sadat's initiative was bitterly condemned, particularly when Israel delayed cooperating in a resolution of the Palestinian problem. In the last month of his life Sadat took sudden action against opposition elements in his own country. He spoke of a plot, arising from religious fundamentalists, and ordered the arrest of about 1,500 people.

On 6 October 1981, Anwar Sadat reviewed the troops on the anniversary of the Yom Kippur War. A vehicle veered out of the marching column, uniformed men stormed the tribune where Sadat and his colleagues and guests stood, threw hand grenades and fired with machine guns. There were 38 wounded and 11 dead, among them Anwar Sadat.